What people are saying about *Executive Presence*:

Dr. Neillie is an exemplary speaker. We've had him present to our teams several times, and we've never been disappointed. He knows how to capture an audience's attention and communicate in such a way that there is practical, personal application for each person in the room. I've listened to many speakers and trainers over the years; Dr. Neillie is the best of the best. - Rob Moore, Executive Director of Global Sales, Orthopaedics & Portable Medical, Greatbatch Medical

In my business, it is not enough to know your stuff. You have to be able to communicate with clarity and conviction. Andy has been a great help to me as I've worked on my own brand of Executive Presence. I really appreciate his practical tips as well as his ability to both recognize my existing skills and challenge me to grow as a leader and communicator. - Eric Heeder, Corporate Operations Manager, The Rockbridge Group

No time to practice for your sales presentation?
Rushed so you'll just "go with what you have used before?"
Thinking you'll figure it out when you are in the meeting?
Compelled to send that email out before you end the day?

Are you kidding me?! In a recent conversation with a Senior Vice President of Cisco, I was reminded of how critical our preparation, word choices, and brevity must be—for big and little communication. This executive shared with me his best practice for gaining attention in an email: "As few words as possible because I have to assume the recipient won't read past 'one screen, and one swipe' on his/her mobile device."

To get any action agreed to and executed internally or external — whether verbally or written — my communication has to be strategic in wording, concise and clear in the call to action, and express obvious and authentic benefit for the other parties involved. Want that? Need that? Show me any business person today who doesn't think his/her communication could be stronger, better, and shorter. If that's you, then this book contains the necessary processes and tips to achieve what I call "must-have-to-win best practices of communication."

Dr. Andy Neillie understands these processes and tips; he lives them out and he trains others to do so. I'm privileged to have worked with Andy and to have experienced for myself his powerful communication in leading workshops for the smartest, most-driven sales teams at Cisco. Whether he is facilitating a formal presentation — commanding a large room of very short-attention-spanned high-tech executives — or motivating and training a small group of professionals to improve their own communication skills for an impending real-deal sales opportunity, Andy's authenticity, expertise and candor is central to his communication coaching.

There is just no way that these attributes woven through this book won't impact you in your professional and personal communication. Indeed, he has helped scores of emerging executives at Cisco Systems improve their ability to say things well, say things briefly and line up their non-verbal communication so it is in sync with their words. After implementing suggestions from Andy, many of my peers found increased success and better opportunities in front of them. They developed their own brand of executive presence, and it paid off for them in increased business success and improved career advancement.

I'm so pleased Andy has taken the time to capture key elements that will allow each of us to gain the respect and attention of the people we work with and seek to influence. The concepts in this book have the ability to help anyone improve their communication and executive presence. My hope is that you will benefit from his insights as much as I have.
- Gene Kent, Regional Manager, Cisco Systems

EXECUTIVE PRESENCE

Golden Rules for Executives, Managers, and Leaders to Maintain Authority
Under Pressure, Communicate Confidence, and Own Any Room

DR. ANDY NEILLIE

DEDICATION

To Lynn, who's been coaching me for more than 30 years. Your "critical eye without a critical spirit" has taught me so much, not just about doing better presentations, but also about life. Here's to the next 30 years of owning the room together.

FOREWORD

"He commanded the room."

"She had a way with words."

"His presentation was very impressive."

"As soon as he walked in, we all knew who was in charge."

In my work with business executives across North America and worldwide, I'm continually reminded that Executive Presence is both real and vital. Corporate CEOs, VPs, Directors and Managers, along with the owners and leaders of small — and medium-sized businesses and non-profits, need to know how to influence the people around and under them. Whether they are making a formal presentation, using slides and visuals in front of a room of hundreds, or simply leading a small meeting in a conference room, those who are effective make it appear effortless. In reality, developing and displaying Executive Presence is something that takes both time and focused energy.

The good news is that Executive Presence can be learned. While we may think that some people are born extroverts who always know the right way to say the right thing and get others to follow them naturally, I've seen introverts and people who are tremendously nervous presenting learn to lead articulately. The skills and behaviors of Executive Presence are available to all of us.

To that end, my aim is that this book will provide a simple-and-robust tool kit for leaders and emerging leaders who know they need to improve their Executive Presence. Do you want to command the room? Do you know you need a way with words? Do you want to be remembered for making impressive presentations that call others to action? Do you want to give others confidence because you are in charge? If so, the ideas and best practices in this book are for you!

- *Dr. Andy Neillie Austin, Texas*

January, 2015

INTRODUCTION

No time to practice for your sales presentation? Rushed so you'll just "go with what you have used before"? Thinking you'll figure it out when you are in the meeting? Compelled to send that email out before you end the day?

Are you kidding me?! In a recent conversation with a Senior Vice President of Cisco, I was reminded of how critical our preparation, word choices, and brevity must be — for big and little communication. This executive shared with me his best practice for gaining attention in an email: "As few words as possible because I have to assume the recipient won't read past 'one screen and one swipe' on his/her mobile device."

To get any action agreed to and executed internally or externally — whether verbally or written — my communication has to be strategic in wording, concise, and clear in the call to action, and it must express obvious and authentic benefit for the other parties involved. Want that? Need that? Show me any business person today who doesn't think his/her communication could be stronger, better, and shorter. If that's you, this book contains the necessary processes and tips to achieve what I call "must-have-to-win, best practices of communication."

Dr. Andy Neillie understands these processes and tips; he lives them and trains others to do so as well. I'm privileged to have worked with Andy and to have experienced for myself his powerful communication in leading workshops for the smartest, most-driven sales teams at Cisco. Whether he is facilitating a formal presentation — commanding a large room of very short-attention-spanned high-tech executives — or motivating and training a small group of professionals to improve their own communication skills for an impending real-deal sales opportunity, Andy's authenticity, expertise, and candor is central to his communication coaching.

There is just no way that these attributes, woven through this book, won't impact you in your professional and personal communication. Indeed, he has helped scores of emerging executives at Cisco Systems improve their ability to say things well, say things briefly, and line up their non-verbal communication so it is in sync with their words. After implementing suggestions from Andy, many of my peers found increased success and better opportunities in front of them. They developed their own brand of executive presence, and it paid off for them in increased business success and improved career advancement.

I'm so pleased Andy has taken the time to capture key elements that will allow each of us to gain the respect and attention of the people we work with and seek to influence. The concepts in this book have the ability to help anyone improve their communication and executive presence. My hope is that you will benefit from his insights as much as I have.

Gene Kent, Regional Manager, Cisco Systems, Inc.

TABLE OF CONTENTS

Part I – Prepare for Success

Part II – Communication Skills

Part III – Practice Makes Perfect

Part IV – Exuding Confidence

Part V – Commanding Authority

Part VI – Owning the Room (Presentation Skills)

Part VII – Bring It All Home

·

PART I

Prepare for Success

Chapter 1: Work Hard

"Nothing ever comes to one, that is worth having,
except as a result of hard work."
— **Booker T. Washington**

Anyone can develop an executive presence and lead. Repeat that to yourself. Anyone can lead, and all it takes to be successful is to work hard. You may think that "working hard" is a given for preparing for success, but what exactly does it mean? Does it mean just doing your best within those standard eight hours at work per day? No. To work hard, to be successful, you need to always be thinking in the back of your mind about what you can do to improve.

Many people think of work as dull and exhausting, but have you ever noticed that the most successful people in the world love working? They go above and beyond, even when they're famous, because they like working. It's fun and rewarding.

If you want to improve something, especially yourself, what do you do?

You seek feedback from other people. After all, you can't know for sure if that hard work has actually paid off unless you hear the opinion of other people. This goes for anything, whether it is a skill you want to practice or developing your presence.

Think about the last time you genuinely worked hard on something. How did you feel? Usually, you feel pretty good about yourself, maybe even proud that you accomplished something great because you put time and effort into it. Now apply this to creating and maintaining a solid, strong executive presence. You want to be confident, positive, and respected. You want to exude an air of authority that people are attracted to, and not intimidated by. You want to be a role model.

"Working hard" seems like a vague direction, which is why you need to tailor it to your definition of success. In order to make the most of your hard work, you have to think about what you want to achieve and how you define success. If you go to the gym and want to tone your arms, but only exercise your legs, then that hard work isn't contributing to your success. Similarly, in business, if you want to "work out" your personality, you can't focus all of your hard work into presentations.

Now comes the fun part. What can you do to work hard and improve?

- Define your vision of success.

- Set goals: a large goal for yourself (such as attaining an impressive executive presence), and smaller goals to reach that large goal.

- Think to yourself, "What can I do today that will bring me closer to achieving one of my goals?"

- Think outside the box or, in this case, the eight-hour workday. Run your ideas by your family, your friends, or, better yet, complete strangers and have them make suggestions.

- Create a timeline: setting personal deadlines will ensure that you take action and actively work toward your goal, instead of just dreaming.

Remember, only you are in charge of yourself. If you work hard and maintain a positive attitude, you will find success. Working hard should bring you happiness, not stress. Yes, there will be obstacles, but, if you handle them with maturity, you can overcome them. That shows discipline, and the result is a better, stronger, and more confident you.

Chapter 2: Listen Well

*"Wisdom is the reward you get for a lifetime of
listening when you'd have preferred to talk."*
— Doug Larson

Executive presence requires the ability to listen and to listen well.
When you think of the best presenters, managers, and leaders, do you
think of individuals who seem to naturally know how to light up a
room with their presentation skills? Do they captivate people with their way
with words, and turn their vision into something others can visualize for
themselves and a plan they want in on before leaving the room? We picture
great leaders as great orators. But people with executive presence are also
people who listen. Before you can walk into a room and impress people with
a knockout presentation or calm an employee that comes to you for advice,
you must consider your ability to listen just as important as your ability to
communicate.

At this point, you might be thinking: what? I worked hard to figure out what I want to say and these people are here to listen to me. Why should I take the time to listen to others in my own presentation or in a conversation where a person wants my advice?

While people came to hear your ideas, you are not the only mind in the room. The person sitting across from you holds questions, thoughts, and feelings worthy of being heard. Along with working hard, communicating clearly, and building relationships, the ability to listen well serves you because it will make you someone others want to trust and follow. When you stop to listen, you act as a true leader. You show people that you value them and the knowledge they bring to the table.

Think back to a time when a boss, a manager, or even a teacher, asked your opinion on how to solve a problem. How important did you feel? How excited were you to contribute to the project or to use what you knew to help someone else? Now imagine: how important will you make others feel when you listen to them?

Since listening is a natural skill, we forget it is a vital one. For those of us with the ability to hear, we've spent our whole lives surrounded by sound (but all of us learn by actually listening to the words of others). As a skill, the act of listening reaps rewards. It helps us engage with the moment just as it first helped us communicate with others as babies. We take turns between the role of speaker and audience, watch our audiences' reaction for understanding, and figure out how to share our minds with people outside of ourselves when we focus on listening instead of hearing.

Listening goes beyond the use of our ears. Well-practiced listeners do more than cue into another's use of words in a conversation; they see the other person's appearance, non-verbal communication, and emotional needs. In the world of business, listening well is a skill that you can tap into, refine, and add to your repertoire of abilities as a leader.

How to listen well during a presentation:

- Set aside sufficient time from your presentation for questions. Five minutes may not be sufficient enough for an hour-long presentation, but also too much time for a ten-minute one.

- Practice your presentation ahead of time so you can watch your audience, and not your computer, cue cards, or PowerPoint screen.

- Recognize signs of confusion or disengagement. If you see brows wrinkled in confusion, people slumped in chairs, or eyes staring down the hands of a clock, listen to your audience and respond. Regain their attention and move on, or stop and clarify.

- Realize you can stop talking and allow questions whenever you want. The Q and A segment of a presentation does not need to be reserved for the end.

- Use a clear announcement to inform your audience that you will take questions. This will prepare both you and them to take your respective turns in the Q and A format.

- Begin your formal Q and A by sharing one of the questions you anticipate the audience may be thinking in order to get the ball rolling.

How to listen well in any conversation:
- Take turns in the roles of speaker and audience. You cannot listen to the other person if you are the only one talking.

- Focus your attention on the person and mentally stay in the moment. Now is not the time to think about making tonight's pot roast or check your cell phone.

- Concentrate on the meaning of the words versus the words themselves. Notice discrepancies between verbal and non-verbal communication. If your employee says she is okay with taking on a heavier workload but wrings her hands at the same time, recognize she feels stressed.

- Take written notes, as appropriate.

- Track non-verbal communication to see how people receive your responses. A smile, direct eye contact, or relaxed body posture are great signals this person is with you.

- Ask questions. If you are not sure you understand the other person, request that they clarify what they mean.

- Stay genuine. If a person asks a question or raises a problem you did not anticipate, tell them you had not thought of this before and offer to reach out to them later with more information.

- Follow up with people. Whether you approach someone at the end of the meeting or shoot them an email later, people will see you think their input matters.

As a leader, you trust those you interact with to listen to you; gift them the same respect. When you do, your business will flourish. By incorporating simple strategies to listen well, you will establish trust, build better relationships, and demonstrate your confidence as a leader. You will also benefit from listening to peoples' questions and concerns because you can later incorporate the feedback into your business to make it stronger.

Remember to take the time to truly listen to others. Whether this occurs during a presentation, a small meeting, or through an email conversation, you open up opportunities to show your skills as a leader and how much you value the people around you when you listen well. By doing so, you will gain wisdom from others' input for the benefit of everyone in your business.

Chapter 3: Communicate Clearly

> *"Don't use words too big for the subject. Don't say*
> *infinitely when you mean very; otherwise you'll have*
> *no word left when you want to talk about something*
> *really infinite."*
> — C.S. Lewis

Communication is more than just words pieced together on paper or being presented to an audience. Words should not be forced together last minute just to get something done. They should flow with ease and hold value. Words should be given the time they deserve to make a document or speech more impactful to those reading and listening. Communication is key.

As with any process, there are steps you can take in order to communicate clearly. These steps can be used when leading a small group of people in a work meeting or presenting to hundreds of people filling an auditorium.

Here are some key points to keep in mind:

- Organize your thoughts. The first step in communicating clearly is to organize your own thoughts on the topic being presented. It's helpful to narrow down your ideas to three main topics that you can always come back to if you become flustered and start sidetracking. Writing these three main points on a notecard to hold while talking to your audience will help you keep on track.

- Choose your words wisely. Who will you be communicating with in the upcoming meeting or presentation? You need to profile your audience in order to know how detailed you need to get with your topic. Is every person going to hold the same knowledge as you do on this topic? You want every single audience member to understand your wording and your topic as a whole.

- Remove any and all distractions. Silence your cell phone and place it in your pocket unless you have use for it in your meeting or presentation. The last thing you want is your phone ringing in the middle of an important meeting that could cost you your job. If your gut is telling you it is not a good idea to have it out, then pocket it and guarantee yourself and your audience members a distraction-less presentation.

- Liven your vocals. When you're communicating with an individual or group of people, you want to make the conversation lively rather than monotonous. Capture your audience's attention by raising the pitch of your voice, slowing your speech, and adjusting your volume when transitioning or emphasizing an important point in your speech.

- Make eye contact. Communication isn't limited to your speech; it also includes your body language and eye contact. Those you are communicating with want to know that you care about them and care about their interest in the topic presented. Make eye contact with audience members to let them know this. Don't stare at the back wall for your whole presentation. Many times, your audience members will reassure you with a smile or a nod of the head.

Communicating clearly is one of the most important factors in succeeding and creating an executive presence. By creating a specific, detailed speech, you are leaving no room for misunderstandings or misinterpretations. Communication is what brings communities and diverse backgrounds together. Have confidence in your ability to do so and success will not be far down the road.

Chapter 4: Cultivating a Healthy Culture

"To all the other dreamers out there, don't ever stop or let the world's negativity disenchant you or your spirit. If you surround yourself with love and the right people, anything is possible."
— Adam Green

W ho you spend your time with matters. Think about that friend, you know the one. The one, who, no matter what their life gives them, is unhappy. That one friend who, when you are around them, sucks the energy and life out of you within the first twenty minutes you've spent with them. You cannot change the way they behave, but you can change the way you do. One way to do this is to surround yourself with people who are like-minded.

If you are looking to be effective, look at those negative friends and ask yourself, "Do they have what I want?" Are those people happy with their family, their love life, and their business? Even if they are in a great job position, are they truly happy? However, there are those in positions that you want and who have the life you want to live. To get to that place, you have to start building the lifestyle you want by finding more positive people. Positive people encourage you, support your endeavors, and build you up so that you can achieve your goals.

Is your business stagnant right now? Are the meetings with your employees getting anywhere? Are the jobs that you want completed done in a timely manner? Do people have smiles on their faces in the office when they arrive and wave to you happily on their way out the door? Chances are, if you answered no, your company is not seeking a healthy culture. The culture that motivates rather than deflates people's self-esteem is the culture you want for your company.

It all starts with you. How are you running your life? Your business? In order to build a positive atmosphere, you have to believe that you can create a positive atmosphere. That means focusing on the good that you're putting out into the world. Say you spilt your coffee today; shake it off and start being grateful you were able to have coffee to drink. Or maybe you woke up late. Celebrate the fact that you still showed up to work and dug in right away. Motivate your team in the same way and appreciate the work that they are contributing.

As for building your team to have the same culture, there are a few tips that you should follow in order to create the atmosphere into a healthy, happy company.

- Trust. The members on your team should all trust one another. If you have a team that constantly points fingers and looks to save themselves over another employee, you have a problem. A positive atmosphere is where everyone trusts each other, is willing to work with one another, and accepts fault when they have made a mistake.

- Constructive conflict. In an organization, it seems unusual to want conflict, but that is not the case. Having conflict can be good if it is in a way where people share their own agenda, beliefs, and desires. In a positive atmosphere, they must consider the needs of each other over the needs of themselves.

- Accountability. This one is probably one of the most important pieces. A good team keeps each other accountable to finish their work in a timely manner. Your team is only as good as your weakest member, so what is the rest of the team doing to make sure that weak link understands the project as well?

- Focus. All team members must be focused on the team's best interest and not themselves. Make sure to keep them focused with motivation and positive support.

In the end, cultivating a healthy atmosphere in your life and business starts with you. What are you doing to change the way the rest of the company interacts with one another? Do not tolerate the people who cannot accept the positive culture you build, and make sure to lead in a way that is positive and motivating to others.

Chapter 5: Seek Clearer Focus

"If a man does not know to what port he is steering,
no wind is favorable to him."
— Seneca

If you want to lead, you have to focus on what you want. Remember that. If you focus, you can do anything. Clear focus is a lot more complex than it seems. Does focus mean single-mindedly devoting yourself to one task until it's completed? No. To succeed you have to see the big picture. Focus on one thing at a time, but you have to have a plan. Before you can focus on what you want, you have to know what you want.

Anyone can live one day at a time. But is that the best way to live? If you want to lead effectively, you need to know what you're living for. You need to know what goal you're working towards.

Think about the last time you worked steadily to achieve a specific purpose. Think about the last time you made a careful plan and saw it through. Now think about the last thing you did on the spur of the moment.

Think of something you threw together just to have it done. Which of these things turned out better — the plan or what you did on the fly? Which one were you more proud of?

Focus isn't always easy, but it's worth the trouble. If you can focus on what you want and how to acquire it, your work will move faster. It will turn out better. You'll have a bigger impact on others, you'll be more confident, and you'll have fewer things to worry about in life.

Anyone can lead. You just need to know where you're leading people, and why. It's easy to get distracted, but in the long run that's going to hurt you. You can't forget what you're leading for. Don't lose sight of your destination.

So how do you achieve clear focus?

- Evaluate where you are now, and decide exactly where you want to go.

- Make a long-term goal for yourself or your business.

- Make short-term objectives that will add up to bring you where you want to be.

- Know your priorities.

- Make sure anyone else involved knows the priorities.

- Make sure they all have the same/compatible long-term goals.

- Know exactly what success looks like for you.

- Take things one day at a time, and don't take on too much, but make sure you're always working towards that long-term goal.

- Don't devote all of your focus and energy to one area. Pay attention to individual issues, but don't lose sight of the forest for the trees. You have to see the whole picture.

Remember, with hard work and clear focus, you can do anything. Don't make vague plans, and don't distract yourself. Know what you want, know how to get it, and it's yours.

Chapter 6: Building Relationships

*"The most important single ingredient in the formula
of success is knowing how to get along with people."*
— Theodore Roosevelt

W hole books have been written on how to build better relationships. It is a skill that is crucially important in building success. The previous chapters in this section lead up to building a better business and personal relationships.

Trust is the key to building a solid foundation for a relationship. How do you build trust? You establish trust by familiarizing yourself with another person, discovering what they want and need, and working hard, within your power, to give it to them. It's a tough practice, but not rocket science.

We are all driven by needs and wants. Intrinsically, it is how we are wired. In order for us to earn the right to have deep, meaningful relationships with the people we want to influence, we need to live out the four pillars of trust-building: character, competence, consistency, and connection.

Character has to do with "who you are when no one is watching." Are you a person of high moral character? Are you mature and even-tempered? Do you have an innate sense of honesty and fairness? Stephen Covey, the well-known author of Seven Habits of Highly Effective People and a number of other best-selling business books, once said, "People are hired for their competence, but fired for their character." How true! What are you doing to develop and demonstrate your character to the people around you? Your relationships will only be as deep as the trust others have for you, based on their opinion of your character.

However, character alone is not enough — if you are going to build and sustain deep, meaningful relationships, you also need to be a person of high competence. Indeed, if you are lacking in competence but are not honest about your abilities and short-comings, it immediately reflects on your character as well. There is an ancient proverb that says, "Do you see a man who is skillful in his work? He will serve before kings, he will not serve before common men." That is the power of competence — when you do things well people respect you, and your ability to build and sustain relationships is enhanced.

The third key factor in building trust is consistency. With consistency, you need to think about two things. First of all, are you diligent? Do you show up when you say you are going to show up? Can people count on your word? If so, you are demonstrating consistency. Secondly, are you even-keeled? That is, are you not prone to fits of anger or depression? A key factor in building relationships and earning trust is proving to others that you are not moody or overly impacted by your circumstances. While it is true that leaders should be emotional, the key question is: who is in charge — you, or your emotions? A mature, influential person who builds deep, lasting relationships does so in part because they are in charge of their emotions: their friends and co-workers know they are consistent.

The final pillar to building trust is the ability to connect. Are you practicing the good communication skills we discuss throughout this book? Are you other-oriented? Do you work to have cultural sensitivity when you are traveling, or working with individuals or a team that may not be from the same background as you? Do you recognize that you need consistent, regular communication? You may consider yourself to be highly worthy of trust but, if the people you are trying to build relationships with feel like they rarely hear from you or interact with you — that is, if they feel they are not connected to you — they won't let you build deep, mutually beneficial work or personal relationships.

Building deep, lasting relationships will be one of the main success factors in extending your executive presence. To do so, you must be a person of high character, with strong competence, who is consistent and works to connect with those you desire to influence.

Chapter 7: Maintain Balance

*"No person, no place, and no thing has any power
over us, for 'we' are the only thinkers in our mind.
When we create peace and harmony and balance in
our minds, we will find it in our lives."*
— **Louise L. Hay**

Despite appointments, errands, household duties, and family life, the key to a successful, happy life is maintaining balance in every area of your life. Many times, you may think that one area should be sacrificed for another, but this certainly isn't true. Instead, finding the right sort of moderation is your best bet.

One of the main ways to achieve this balance is to stay organized in every facet of your life. Having a clear plan, a solid focus, and interpersonal skills that combine listening and excellent communication is one of the best ways to create the sort of balance that will ultimately provide you with a healthy, successful life both at work and at home. Instead of pushing away a few tasks that may not seem as important, make sure to begin each and every week with a plan that encompasses everything you need to get done.

Whether it's a file on your computer, a planner, or a list of duties you type into your phone, greeting each week with a calm and collected mindset is incredibly important.

Life in itself is a sort of balancing act, and being able to handle crises that may arise (and ultimately will) will allow you to maintain balance even in the most stressful situations.

Let's say that an employee comes to you with a problem and, due to this problem, has not been able to finish a task on time. Instead of jumping to conclusions, or getting angry, find a time that week to schedule a brief chat with them, so that you both can hash out the details and come to a better, clearer conclusion. Not only will this maintain a personal balance between you and your employee, but it will also show your employee that you aren't just a title, but a human being that cares about their personal life. Further, this will only add fuel to your employee's commitment to their job, and, in the long run, benefit your work balance.

However, this isn't to say that you should sacrifice duty for personal relationships altogether. Instead, it's just a reminder to seek harmony amongst your team in order to maintain the finely tuned structure of your work environment.

Let's review the tips for keeping your life in balance:

- Make a point to get to know your employees and/or co-workers by using your listening and communication skills.

- Take an interest in their lives, but still respect personal boundaries in regards to office environment.

- Maintain a clear focus of what you can feasibly achieve each week.

- Spend time mapping out your work schedule, and build in points of time that you will need for personal activities, errands, and duties.

Maintaining your cool is the key to this balancing act, and implementing the four things above will only further your ability to achieve what is necessary during your week.

PART II

Communication Skills

Chapter 8: Think About It

"Think twice before you speak, because your words
and influence will plant the seed of either success or
failure in the mind of another."
— Napoleon Hill

Y ou have probably heard the phrase "Think before you act" multiple
times throughout your life. As a leader, this phrase is more
important than ever, because you need to demonstrate that you can
communicate clearly without losing your cool. Communicating effectively
means you have to give consideration to every thought that enters your mind,
and then sweep through for the truly great ideas that will best represent you
and build an impeccable reputation.

To be an inspiring leader, you need to communicate your ideas clearly,
but if you don't think about what you want to communicate, you'll catch
yourself dancing around the topic and confusing your employees or your
clients. That is something you definitely want to avoid, so you need to be
articulate.

Communicating, whether it is an important presentation for a client or an email to an employee, requires a careful process that will be covered throughout "Part II," but begins with thinking. In fact, most of the topics covered in this section will be factored into your thinking.

You must:

- Sit down and set aside time to pull together your ideas.

- Determine your audience (a client, employee, etc.).

- Gather the best ideas and structure them so they form cohesive points.

- Think about the best way to communicate the information you have, through email, text, paper, or presentation.

- Rehearse your ideas, both in your head and aloud, so that you don't leave out an important idea.

- Listen to others so you can improve upon your ideas and potentially think about an idea from a different angle.

- Use your past experiences, reflect on them, and incorporate them into your future thought process to better communicate.

- Repeat the process.

What's the idea here? It is this: you're never done with the thinking process. No matter what happens, even if you become adept at communicating, there will always be something you can improve for next time. That's not a bad thing. It's what keeps you going and gives you something to look forward to.

When communicating, it is crucial to first determine your audience. You probably won't address your client in the same manner as your family, or vice versa. The way you talk to your audience could make or break the relationship; that's why you're communicating, to build relationships.

Thinking before you speak, write, or act is what allows you to present yourself in a manner that will build and strengthen your relationship.

Thinking also prepares you for most things. Put yourself in your client's or employee's shoes. What would he or she ask? Write down a list of questions you would potentially have if you were listening to the presentation or on the receiving side of the email. Then, once you've combed your brain, answer each and every question. You might even find something to add to your presentation that you hadn't previously thought of.

You should also consider that the way you think will vary depending on the form of communication. Written communication is simpler than face-to-face communication in the sense that you send it out and don't have an immediate reaction. In a presentation or other meeting, you need to think about your tone. Are you meeting a prospective client? Then you probably want to speak in an open and friendly manner that says you are open to their ideas and are willing to work closely to achieve a common goal. If it's a serious business meeting, you still want to maintain that positivity, but also remain firm and direct.

Each time you communicate, check in with yourself and ask deeper questions about your communications styles and preferences. If you prefer to communicate through email, think about why you do. Ask yourself if that means you have to brush up on your face-to-face communication. Likewise, if you prefer speaking to a group to writing messages, think about what makes you hesitate, and move on from there. Above all, the importance of thinking before you communicate is so that you avoid confusion. You are a leader. Your words have influence.

Chapter 9: Structure It

"Communication works for those who work at it."
— John Powell

Similar to the idea that there is no correct or incorrect way to structure leadership in your company, there is no single right or wrong way to structure communication when it comes to your business. Instead, the approach you take depends on the needs of your business and the vision you hold for it. No matter your role in a business, the way you approach communication as a leader sets the stage for those who follow you. The communication structure you select must align itself with the goals for your business, and it will benefit your business to find the right structure for you.

In order to begin to evaluate what structure you need, take time to examine what you currently use in your business and the present obstacles you face when it comes to communication. Perhaps you've built a flexible environment where employees spark informal conversations with managers, or clients stop by for a cup of coffee on a regular basis. On the other end of the spectrum, your communication structure may have you as a leader that conveys messages to managers to pass further down the chain. Ultimately, the question to ask is: does your current structure help or hinder you?

Be honest. If you have never intentionally established a communication structure for your business before, seize this moment and make the decision as a leader in your workspace to do so. If your current structure doesn't work or is lacking, you may need to refine a part of your process. Greet the opportunity to make a change to better yourself and your business.

Here are some basic questions to help you construct a communication structure to fit your unique needs:

- What message will you share? Your overall message will become the focus of your communication structure and should represent you and what you want to convey to others about your business and employees. It may be helpful to think about your business goals and what outcomes you want to achieve as you pinpoint the message you wish to share.

- Who is your audience? You would not talk to a teacher the same way as your sibling; likewise, you will want to adjust your communication approach based on your intended audience. Use your knowledge of an audience to understand their needs. If your audience consists of customers, divide them into recent, present, and current customers, and decide how to adjust your message to reach each type.

- What must they know? Identifying your audience will allow you to take your overall message and tailor it into key messages, or points, to reach that specific group of people. Pick no more than four or five key messages that will lead your audience to the goal you want to achieve without confusing them with too much information.

- What is the reason behind communicating? Assessing why the communication is going to take place will better prepare you to meet with your audience. If a recent sales meeting did not go well, you will want to select key messages to calm your audience. On the other hand, if you are meeting with a prospective client at a nearby cafe, you can elect to bring along a brochure that highlights your business's strengths and leave the projector screen behind.

- Which communication techniques best fit the situation? You already possess a toolkit full of different techniques to reach out to different people. Ready with the knowledge of the audience you will engage with, you can select the best method to contact them, which can be anything from more traditional contact (such as a phone call, letter, or newspaper advertisement) to contact that uses technology (such as email, social media forums, or a Skype call). Pick the best tool to match your audience's communication preferences.

- How will you determine success? In order to decide if your communication structure works effectively, you must put a measurement system in place to gauge its success. Depending on your needs, this can range from formal measures (such as an evaluation form, sales reports, or customer records) to informal measures (such as a sticky note tally of how many employees submitted their sick-time requests in the new system versus the old one). What is important here is that determining how well your communication was received should become part of your structured approach.

Use the answers you find to these questions to determine the communication structure you want to either implement or strengthen, and then initiate your plan. Inform your employees that you expect them to follow a new communication structure and explain how these changes will help you achieve your goals and deliver your message as a business. Stay supportive by being friendly and approachable, and allow your employees to ask questions. Most important, identify and share moments as you see the structure you implement better your business so you can celebrate your efforts.

Like all change, expect the learning pains that accompany periods of transition. The greater the change, the more difficult the transition may be initially — but it will be worth it. In order to support those working for you, you can adopt an open-door policy, hold a meeting, or use an announcement around the office to reassure your employees that you are there for them to discuss the changes and remind them how the process will bring you all closer to your business goals.

You will discover that the communication structure you utilize bolsters your business when it helps your company achieve its goals, when it compliments your preferences and abilities as a leader, and when it suits your employees and business interactions. As a leader, remember to model the communication structure you establish for your business. Each time you communicate, you should mentally check yourself to ensure that you deliver your message. By staying present in the moment at hand, your communication skills will shine and you will empower both yourself and the people you communicate with.

Chapter 10: Different Communication Styles

"Nothing stings quite like an unanswered text message."
— Paula Stokes

I'm sure you've felt it. The anger or disappointment washing over you when it's an hour later and someone still hasn't replied to your last text. Isn't the whole idea of communication giving and receiving information? Whether you are writing an email or sending a quick text message, the receiver expects a response, especially in today's high-speed society.

However, emails and text messages hold different standards in regards to communication. Below are some differences you should take into account when deciding what should be included in an email versus a text message.

Formatting an email:

- Salutation: begin by addressing the recipient in an appropriate manner. When emailing someone familiar to you, it is acceptable to say "hi" and address them by their given name. If, however, you are writing to a superior, a client, or individual you don't know as well, you should begin with "Dear [Mr./Ms./Mrs. Last Name]."

- Body: you then have your message body, where you should include the main points needed to get the whole message across. Start your body paragraph(s) with an interesting and important fact about the topic you are writing about. This should hook the reader.

- Complimentary close: when ending your email, you want to be polite with your word choice. Saying "Goodbye" wouldn't settle nicely with the reader. The reader wants to know that you respect his or her position. Try using, "Sincerely yours," "Cordially yours," or "Respectfully yours."

- Signature: make sure to include your full name and contact information at the bottom of your email. This should include your title in the company, as well as a professional phone number and email the recipient can use to reach you.

In a text message, you may find yourself being more informal than when you're writing an email. In today's society, this is okay. Text messages are more conversational and shorter than emails. You will notice how the parts of a text message differ from the parts of an email.

Formatting a text message:

- Salutation: since this is a more informal way of corresponding with another, your wording tends to be less professional. However, you still want to acknowledge the person you are texting, whether it's a friendly co-worker or the vice president of the company. Be sure to greet your recipient with his or her name to begin the message.

- Body: you will notice that the body of your text message is much shorter than the body of your email. Make your text message short and to the point. If you find yourself writing paragraphs of text, you may want to consider writing an email to the recipient instead.

- Complimentary close: the closing for a text message still needs to be respectful. Most of the time, a text message will close saying, "Thank you," or, "See you tomorrow." This closing will depend on the type of message you are trying to get across.

- Signature: it is important to use your full name when sending a text message. The recipient may or may not have you in his or her contact list. This saves time for the recipient, so he or she does not have to send a message back asking who sent them a message.

There may be times when neither an email nor a text message is suitable for your purpose. In very formal situations, it may be necessary to send a letter. These should include the components of an email, like the salutation, message body, complimentary close, and signature. In addition, it should begin with a heading (your name and address), the date, and an inside address (the recipient's name and address).

Although the formats for an email, text message, and letter differ, you want to make sure to stay consistent for formality and grammar. There is no harm in double-checking over your word choice and sentence structure before pressing the send button or sealing the envelope. If the recipient sends you a response, analyze whether a reply is needed. Technology is changing rapidly, and knowing the difference in communication styles for all forms of communication is essential to creating and maintaining an executive presence in your business.

Chapter 11: Deliver It

*"You can have brilliant ideas, but if you
can't get them across, your ideas won't
get you anywhere."*
— Lee Iacocca

D o you find speaking to an audience difficult? Do you get awkward
or nervous, word things poorly, or even speak too aggressively?
Communication is a vital part of leadership, and if you want to
communicate well, you have to know how to deliver.

Be conscious of how you're delivering your message, whether it's to
a large audience or just one or two people, face to face, by phone, or by
email. It doesn't matter what you're saying — if you don't come off well,
no one will listen. We've all watched people stumble through presentations
they aren't prepared for, or read emails worded so poorly we have no idea
what the sender intended to say. Our thoughts have wandered during these
presentations, and often we don't even try to parse confusing messages.
You don't want any of your communications to look like this, and it can be

avoided by putting deliberate effort into your delivery.

This has to do with body language and tone, but what is absolutely essential is sticking to the things people want to hear. Don't sugarcoat anything, but keep it interesting. Do we want to hear about all of the precise and complex mathematics that went into the information you're presenting? Not unless we're all engineers. Do we want to wait for ten minutes while you try to remember if this particular anecdote occurred on the way to or the way from Sweden? No. Is anyone going to pay attention to your elaborate tangent on clams in a speech about clothing production? Of course not.

A lot of elements go into a good delivery. Here are a few to start:

- Know your audience. Different people are inclined to listen to different things and process information in different ways. Different people will have different levels of knowledge on any given topic.

- Practice first.

- Structure what you're saying carefully. Make it flow.

- Be careful with the fillers. No one wants to hear "um" every three words. Know beforehand what you want to say, and say it. If you need time to think, just think. A moment of silence is much better than a moment of useless filler words.

- Be honest, even if the truth isn't great to hear. There's no point in standing up and delivering a lie.

- Be concise. Don't let irrelevant details bog you down. Tell people what they need to know.

- Stay calm. Everyone recognizes nervous ticks, and whether it's crossing your arms, biting your nails, or shoving hands in your pockets, no one wants to see you up there suffering.

- Maintain eye contact when possible.

- Good posture is important.

- Watch your tone. Don't sound too dry and technical. Be passionate. Be funny. Do it in whatever way works best for you, but be entertaining. Make people want to listen.

- Keep on moving. Don't get stuck on one point, don't pause for too long, and don't let technical difficulties slow you down. (Sometimes this last one is inevitable, but keep going if you can.)

Communication is hard, but, with hard work and practice, your delivery can be exceptional.

Chapter 12: Listen Up

*"The ear of the leader must ring with
the voices of the people."*
—Woodrow Wilson

Remember, communication goes both ways. It doesn't matter how good you are at expressing yourself — if you want to be an effective leader, you have to listen, too. Leaders have to know what their followers want. You can't lead anybody anywhere if you don't know where they're expecting to go, why they want to be there, and what they want when they reach their destinations.

You need to be prepared to answer questions and address concerns, but that's only the beginning. Think about work. Think about school. Remember sitting at a desk and raising your hand, waiting until the teacher was ready to listen? Have you ever seen a flaw in what was being done, and been unable to fix it because whoever was in charge didn't listen or take you seriously?

Think about that now. Remember how you felt. Angry? Inadequate? You don't want people you communicate with to feel that way, and you don't want to deal with a project failing because you ignored the person who saw the problems. Leadership isn't just fifteen minutes of Q&A at the end of a speech. Leadership is a conversation.

Create relationships with the people you work with. Take those relationships beyond the workplace — people are much more willing to be led by someone who knows the ages of their kids and the names of their pets. And it holds you accountable. People will be more comfortable calling you out on something you shouldn't do if they feel like they know you.

Don't be afraid to ask for help. Find people with different perspectives. Be open to new ideas. You can't possibly know everything, so look out for people who can fill the gaps in your knowledge. Pay attention to what's going on around you, and not just what you're hearing. Find new ways to listen. People communicate in hundreds of ways without ever opening their mouths, so you need to know what they're saying with their body language, or in memos and emails, too.

Listening can be complicated, and it doesn't come easily to everyone. But you can learn.

Here are a few tips to get you started:

- Make eye contact. Nod, smile, and make other appropriate nonverbal responses while someone else has the floor.

- Maintain control of the discussion, but make sure that all the other voices are heard.

- Make sure everyone feels included.

- Don't get distracted when other people are speaking.

- Don't interrupt. If you disagree with someone, wait until they're done to say so and do it politely.

- Reply with helpful feedback, if necessary. Clarify and summarize the speaker's points.

- If you don't have the answer to a question, be honest.

- Be patient, respectful, and understanding.

Listening doesn't always come naturally to leaders, but, if you really want to be great at what you do, it's absolutely vital. Just be open, remember that you're never in this alone, and your communication skills will improve in leaps and bounds.

Chapter 13: Improve Your Communication

*"Wise men speak because they have
something to say; Fools because they
have to say something."*
—Plato

Communication is key to success in life. In Chapter 6, I talked about how building a relationship with people is one of the most important keys to success, right? Well, you can build a relationship by bettering your communication skills. By communicating with a person, you begin to understand more about what other people want. When you give other people what they want, they will in turn give you what you want. It's a cycle of give and take. Give them a reward, and you are rewarded.

There are some key ways to change how you communicate, and, with practice, you can and will communicate better.

Listed here are some of the simplest ways to improve your communication skills:

- Body language. Body language and non-verbal cues can change a situation in a hurry. You mention to the person you are talking to that you are open and ready to discuss anything they want to talk about, but you have your arms crossed, or you cannot make eye contact. If you want to be open, your body needs to show it just as much as the words coming out of your mouth. When getting ready to talk to a person, remember to have your arms open, a smile on your face, and a poised posture.

- Engage. Engaging with the person you are talking to speaks volumes. Make that person feel special and listen to what he or she has to say. Leave yourself out of the equation and keep him or her talking. If he or she mentions an interest, job, hobby, or a family member, say, "Tell me more about…." Then listen again and ask more questions. Write things down if you know you will forget. Ask them follow-ups from the things they said to you in a previous conversation.

- Tell your Story. Your story can be powerful, and a great way to communicate with another person. Relate to the person next to you by telling your story. You've not only made yourself more human, but you have connected on a level that most people are not comfortable with. If you have failed, show it. People want to know more that you are real, not fake. Not everyone is a rock star all the time. Your failures make you relatable and a person that people can work with.

- Focus. Focusing on the other person, without distractions, is one of the deepest signs of respect. The person across from you, next to you, or on the phone, is the only thing that should matter during the time you are with them. Put away your cell phone. Turn it off and put it in your bag. Leave it in the car. Get off your computer when on an important conference call. Focus on what you are doing with that person at that time. The phone can wait. If you know an emergency is coming up, instead of leaving your phone out with you, reschedule for a time when it will be better and you can spare your full attention.

- Listen. Listening is the most important skill you can learn. Everyone wants to know they are being heard. Active listening can be the hardest skill to learn, but it is vital. If you don't listen to the people you are talking to, you do not value them. You are telling them that they are not important enough or worth your time. Not only is it rude, but it is also downright selfish. Not listening will get you nowhere. So, hone that skill and pay attention when you are talking to someone. It will help you greatly.

Improving your communication skills will be an ongoing task that you need to keep up on. In order to do that, you must practice all the time. Find which parts of communication you are good at and really think about the communication skills you are bad at. If you know you need to listen better, work on it. Figure out what hinders you and why you do not listen well. If you know checking your cellphone is a problem when you are out, leave it in the car.

Practice telling your story both in writing and speaking. There are an abundance of classes online and free materials to help you craft your story better. Make sure to ask deeper questions when talking to someone. Remember the phrase, "Tell me more." Always keep your body language open and ready to engage in a powerful conversation. Work on these skills one at a time and you will communicate better.

Chapter 14: Try Again

*"My world changed when I started focusing on
the skills and made the commitment to practice,
practice, practice, until I mastered them."*
—Eric Worre

With anything in life, practice is key. Whether it's a hobby, a goal, such as running a marathon, or, more specifically, communicating, nothing is instantaneous; perfecting your techniques through practice is the only way to achieve results.

Two things that are directly linked to success in regards to practicing are frequency and feedback. Luckily, you have complete control over the frequency — that's entirely up to you. The feedback is also easy to come by, since you will be able to see direct results from your practiced attempts.

We talked a good bit about structure and various communication styles in this section, but, without implementing these every day (in other words, practicing them every day), no amount of planning will get you to where you need to be.

Humans are so diverse, and we communicate in a wide variety of ways. While some people are more skilled with writing, others are far better at vocalizing their thoughts. Luckily, you are surrounded by both types of people, and have a multitude of opportunities to learn the best approaches in terms of communication for all types. Humans are social creatures, and the most basic fabric of our society is one that is deeply ingrained in communication.

One way to go about practicing communication is to break it down, while focusing on specific pieces. This not only allows you to become an expert on every facet of the "skill," but also gives you time to process what you're practicing. This also helps with any sort of overwhelming feelings you might experience when taking on something as weighty as communication.

So, with that being said, here's a break down of what you should be focusing on when practicing your communication skills:

- Repetition. Regardless of failure, you must be able to take a deep breath, brush yourself off, and try, try again.

- Pay attention to the specific skills you are trying to learn. Assess these on your own, and really try to understand what you're practicing.

- Also, pay attention to the feedback you are receiving. People's responses will be a great help for you, and will allow you to work on areas you may be lacking in.

- Keep a sharp eye on your performance and improvement. Take a minute to step back and analyze where you began, and how you are improving.

Anyone can learn to communicate effectively, but it takes patience and the ability to step outside of yourself in order to understand other people. Think of it as the most basic form of psychology — while you may be used to communicating in one way, the person next to you may differ completely.

This isn't bad; it's actually a fantastic learning experience. Understanding people, and taking the time to realize all of the little intricacies that the human personality is made up of will not only further your communicative success, but also render you a more understanding, perceptive, and accepting person.

PART III

Practice Makes Perfect

Chapter 15: Writing It Down

*"Success depends upon previous preparation, and
without such preparation there is
sure to be failure."*
—Confucius

Have you ever had an excellent idea and then forgot about it? We all have. The trick is to write it down. If you have a great thought, the next step is to remember it. Always keep a pencil or pen nearby so you are prepared to write your idea down on anything: a piece of paper, the back of an old letter, a napkin, or even a note on your computer or phone.

We hardly ever remember great ideas if we don't write them down. That's why we have books. That's why we have this book. The act of writing out your ideas gives you clearer focus and allows you to contemplate what you thought deeper than before. Writing gives you a sense of purpose and, as a leader, that's especially helpful when preparing presentations and client meetings. Rehearsing what you want to say boosts your confidence, and writing down what you want to rehearse helps you memorize all of the important topics you want to touch on.

Not only does writing down your ideas cement them, but it also gives you the opportunity to build on it. As your idea stares you in the face, more often than not, a little light bulb will ping over your head, and several more connecting ideas surface.

Stress and anxiety are huge obstacles when preparing for a presentation or meeting. Another benefit to writing your thoughts down is that the space in your mind is freed and reduces that anxiety. Whether you're an extrovert or an introvert, you can always use more breathing room to clear your head and focus on the task at hand.

Writing your ideas out will help organize you. If you don't prepare for your presentation by writing things down, your points will be all over the place and you will circle around, which loses your client's or employees' attention. When you write, you connect the dots and reorganize what you have to say in a clean and orderly format. Doing this will pack your points with more punch.

Practice is certainly made easy when you can refer to notes, and that leads to another inadvertent benefit of writing. Once you free up your mind, you can focus on other tasks. Instead of worrying about your important conference, you can relax and increase your productivity because you've written your thoughts down, rehearsed your presentation, and boosted your confidence.

Writing has also been proven to have psychological health benefits, ones that have been tested again and again to help you in the workplace, and even your personal life.

The benefits of writing are not limited to this list below, but include:

- Improves your mood and well-being, resulting in a more positive work and/or home environment.

- Betters your thinking and communicating, as touched on earlier in this chapter.

- Keeps you quick-witted as you age (think of writing as a bench press for your brain).

- Inspires you to learn as you research your ideas to spice up your presentation.

Go ahead and give writing a try, especially when those perfect thoughts enter your mind! You'll find that it benefits you in more ways than one. The quality of your presentations and other forms of communication will improve, and, if you practice writing daily, it will give you more structure and discipline to focus on what matters most.

Chapter 16: Speaking It Out Loud

"Improvement is achieved by the ripple effect of a few simple changes in approach, attitude, or habit."
—Dale Ludwig and Greg Owen-Boger

Growing up in the West, we learn to sit in front of our birthday cakes, focus our thoughts on a single wish, suck in a full breath, and blow out the burning candles before us. Even though that secret wish matters, we learn to keep it to ourselves and not to share it with others in the room (theoretically, unless someone manages to get us to spill the secret).

As adults, it is important to share our thoughts and ideas with each other, and not to tuck them away within ourselves. Even if you feel at ease at the front of a room talking to others, or if you are someone who considers such a situation as your worst nightmare, the first place to begin bettering your public speaking skills is to remember your opinion matters. Take a moment, right now, to say out loud: "What you say matters."

Once you put in the effort of writing your ideas down, the best way to start gathering confidence in your own voice is to practice speaking it out loud when you are all by yourself. While you will want to practice on a volunteer audience later, at this stage you should find a private space to practice in for your own comfort and remove distractions, so you can focus on the task at hand. At this point, you will want to look at the ideas you wrote down and summarize them into key points for a basic, easy-to-remember outline. This strategy will prove useful for a variety of speaking situations, from an informal meeting that you lead with your employees to an hour-long public speaking event where you are a presenter. An outline will keep your mind focused and boost your confidence because you have already identified what you want to say.

Whatever the event is in which you must speak as a leader, take the time to orally practice your ideas at least two times beforehand. If you find speaking in front of others gives you anxiety, begin your practice session with breathing exercises. Physiologically, nervousness causes an increased heart rate, vascular constriction, and increased adrenaline production. One of the best ways to counteract these effects physically is with the nine-second three-by-three-by-three-by-three breathing practice: Inhale slowly for three seconds, hold a full breath for three seconds, and then exhale slowly for three seconds. Do this three times prior to getting in front of others, and you will experience your body adopting a more relaxed physical state.

Since many of us feel nervous about speaking out loud in front of others, one of the best things you can do is find a way to watch yourself as you practice. Depending on your comfort level, you can practice what you need to say while standing in front of a mirror so you can take in your body language, use of eye contact, and facial gestures as they occur. Others of you may find it more helpful to record yourself on a video camera or even your cellphone for the same effect. Whichever strategy you decide to go with, remember to practice in the manner you will deliver your words (standing up or sitting down) and with a timer. No matter what, do not let yourself engage in a cycle of negative nit-picking! Remind yourself why you are practicing: to improve yourself. There is a difference between giving yourself constructive feedback that you can use to make your next time speaking better and tearing yourself down.

Finally, while you continue to sharpen your speaking skills as you practice, think about how you want others to perceive you. Note the tone of voice you use. If it comes across monotone or insincere, your audience will think you do not want to be with them, even if your words tell them the direct opposite. Keep your voice friendly and practice not talking too fast or too slow. Most important, remind yourself why you are eager to share your ideas in the first place. When you are in a good mood and focused on why your ideas matter and should be shared, your genuine attitude will come across in your voice, and your audience will recognize this and respond positively to it.

Above all, trust the process. You may feel silly and nervous. You may feel awkward, but the time you take to practice saying it out loud is the best time to work through those feelings, instead of when you are standing in front of a group of people. After all, this is your time to learn! Expert speakers plan ahead and practice ahead of time. When you take the time to speak your ideas out loud, you give yourself the chance to find the confidence behind your words and the sound of your voice saying them out loud. When it's time, tell yourself out loud, "You're ready." And then walk into that room a confident leader ready to share your mind with others.

Chapter 17: Find a Practice Audience

"If you have an important point to make, don't try to be subtle or clever. Use a pile driver. Hit the point once. Then come back and hit it again. Then hit it a third time — a tremendous whack."
—Winston S. Churchill

The last thing you want to happen when you walk into the conference room or auditorium is to get in front of a group of people and freeze. Your mind goes blank and seems to forget everything you wrote down last night for today's presentation. Now what?

Hopefully you never have to ask yourself this question. A technique that will help you avoid this is practice. You have your presentation written down, organized, and ready to go. However, you're not ready...at least not yet. You will want to rehearse your speech to yourself a few times, and then in front of a practice audience, to get a feel for what talking in front of a group of people will actually feel like.

Let's take a look into what a practice audience might look like for you, and some tips to help guide you through it more easily:

- Choosing an audience. Your practice audience can include whoever you would like. However, try not to choose people you are completely comfortable around. Think about your future audience, and ask yourself who it is going to consist of. Are these people going to be co-workers, managers, or strangers? Choose your practice audience based on your future audience. See if a couple of your co-workers would be willing to share some of their lunch break listening to your presentation. If not, friends and family members are always great resources for constructive criticism.

- Rehearse individually. Before you practice in front of your chosen audience, rehearse your speech or presentation on your own a few times. Break your presentation into different parts. Focus on rehearsing the first part and once you feel comfortable with the wording and flow, move onto the next part. Do not move onto the next part until you feel comfortable enough to proceed. This will help you memorize certain key points and words to help guide you when you present in front of your future audience.

- Rehearse with practice audience. Now that you've practiced on your own, you'll find yourself more comfortable in front of your practice audience. Now is the time to make mistakes and experiment with emphasizing key parts of your speech. Change the tone and volume of your voice, as mentioned in Chapter 3, to let your audience know this specific part of your speech is important or significant.

- Question and Answer time. Ask your practice audience questions about the presentation you just performed for them. Let them know you would appreciate feedback on the speed, length, and overall clarity of your speech. This will help you make any edits needed before you walk into the meeting or conference room to give your final presentation. Take this feedback as constructive criticism. Do not let this bring your attitude or drive down. Your practice audience is there to help you.

After you rehearse in front of your practice audience, you will notice a weight lifted off your shoulders. This upcoming speech or presentation is no longer as daunting as you first thought it was. This is because you practiced on your own and in front of a trial audience. Your comfort level and your familiarity with your speech will increase, only helping you in the long run. The day of your meeting, you'll notice that standing up and presenting your information is much easier.

Chapter 18: Creating Structure for Comfort

"...why I like timetables, because they make
sure I don't get lost in time."
—Mark Haddon

Juggling a busy work schedule, with multiple appointments scattered throughout the week, as well as life outside of work leads to two things: stress and anger. But the above list doesn't have to lead to stress and anger. Instead, it can lead to control and comfort. There are ways you can balance your busy work life with your even busier weekend life. "How can I do this?" you may ask.

Read below for some helpful strategies:

- Invest in a calendar and an agenda. This is a low, cost-effective way to keep your days organized. If you don't have the desire to spend money on a calendar, simply create a calendar on your computer and print it out. Having a calendar over your workspace, whether it be in your home office or work office, will allow you to keep track of the most important dates regarding work, as well as important dates outside of work. Having an agenda that fits inside your workbook or bag allows you to take quick notes of certain deadlines or times to remember in meetings or on-the-go. The compact size of an agenda is just a plus!

- Create a timetable. Timetables can be created with pen and paper, or you can find a free template to use online. This timetable will hold your whole schedule for the week. It is similar to an agenda; however, it allows you to see hour-by-hour what times are taken and what times are available. Write down the times you have meetings or what times you will be working on a certain project. This timetable will not only serve as a reminder, but will also help you live a more organized life. Timetables aren't limited to just the current week. If you find yourself more comfortable creating a timetable for the coming week, go ahead and create another one. Try not to overwhelm yourself during this process.

- Schedule time for yourself. When creating a timetable, don't forget to schedule time for yourself. This time can be a quick coffee break or an hour-long meditation session. However long it takes to de-stress yourself, block it off. You'll also find it helpful if you block this time off at the same time every day. It is comforting to look down at your timetable and see that "me time" is always scheduled. As important as your career is, your health and well-being are even more important.

Your busy life is no reason to stress. When you stress, your immune system weakens, making you more susceptible to illness. So do away with the clutter and mess of your busy life! Create structure where you never thought structure could exist before. This is all about making you more comfortable with your work and life in order to be more successful in the long run. Don't fret. Just write it down and remember to always make time for yourself.

Chapter 19: Improvising Within Structures

"We are not creatures of circumstance; we are creators of circumstance."
—Benjamin Disraeli

A re you bored by following the same schedule every day? Do you get sick of a meal after eating it three days in a row? Structure is important, but it can also be constricting. Have a structure in place, because without it you'll have chaos and that's never a good way to live. But leave plenty of room for adjustments in that structure, and you should always be ready to shake your approach up a bit. Your plan may be the best possible thing to do right now, but the same solutions won't work for every situation.

Improv can be intimidating — unless what you're leading is a theater troupe. But there's no acting required here. In fact, one of the best ways to improvise within your structure is just to be open and honest. If there's a flaw in your plan that you can fix by trying something new, admit it. If someone new or inexperienced suggests a change that will improve things, make that change. Don't cling to your structure out of pride or fear of something different. Plan ahead, but be ready for anything.

Be creative. Be spontaneous. Take a chance. Occasionally it may backfire, but in the long run it's going to pay off—it'll keep things interesting, keep people out of ruts, and make your leadership more effective and enjoyable for yourself and everyone else.

Communication is key, here. Improvisation tends to involve group work. But even if you're working on your own—when you're giving a speech, for example, or making a presentation—communication skills are essential. You'll need to be able to read people, and you must respond quickly and appropriately.

Often, improvisation involves striking out on your own and ignoring things like precedence, but a few suggestions won't hurt.

- Be aware of your surroundings. Notice the setting, and notice the people around you. Keep an eye out for signs of anger, confusion, or boredom, and adjust accordingly.

- Pay attention to suggestions and reports from others.

- Create an open environment where people feel comfortable communicating honestly.

- Think quickly — be able to switch gears suddenly and creatively.

- Try new things sometimes, just because you can. You never know what might work out.

- Collaborate.

- Don't get angry if someone's new idea doesn't work out as planned— that person will be less likely to share ideas in the future, and they might have come up with something great next time.

- Try building on ideas, rather than criticizing them.

- No second-guessing when you're in a hurry. Do what you need to do right then, and trust that it will all work out.

- Still make plans. You should always have a structure. Just be prepared not to follow it.

- Remember, improvisation is supposed to be fun.

Take chances. Make changes. Improvising can seem like a risk at first, but more often than not, it pays off. Leave room for excitement in your leadership.

Chapter 20: Polishing Your Words

"Much speech is one thing,
well-timed speech is another."
—Sophocles

Once you have your speech together, it is the time to really make it shine. It's one thing to write a speech and practice, but now it's time to make that speech gleam. When getting in front of a crowd, they expect you to be prepared. They want to know that you have the authority and are the expert on the issue you are talking about. So, you've written your speech on paper, notecards, whatever. You have looked through it and have read it out loud. You've made it to this point.

Now it's time to polish those words. Try memorizing parts of it to give yourself more authority. Start with memorizing the opening and closing paragraphs. Practice in front of the mirror to get it down. Make sure if you are memorizing your speech that you have it down with confidence and that you are able to give the speech without relying on your script.

Another good way of polishing your speech is to look deeper at the content. Make sure that the speech you are about to give has a reason "why" behind it. Why does this speech matter? What does this speech tell the audience about the topic you are speaking on? Is there something new in the speech? Do you give a special twist to an old subject? Ask all of these questions to make sure that your speech is relevant. Even pull in others around you to make sure they agree that your speech matters. At this point — take criticism and leave your ego checked at the door. Nothing would be worse than for you to go out on a stage in front of people with a poor script.

Along with the speech itself, this is the time to write your bio and introduction that will accompany it. When the announcer gets up to introduce you, you want to be sure that the introduction they are giving is the introduction that you want. If you have never created an introduction for someone before, your resume can be used as a template.

A good introduction has just a few things:

- Where you are from. The background of where you grew up is an important piece of the introduction. It makes you more relatable to the crowd and adds that human touch.

- Your expertise in the field. What is your speech on? You need to make sure that the person who is introducing you does a good job of making you relevant. They need to have the tools to prove that you are important enough in whatever it is that you are speaking about to have an audience.

- A client testimony. Testimonies are great if you have them, especially if you are in a business that provides services to other people. Proof that your solutions or product work makes you entirely credible in the field of your speech and also gives the story element that always boosts the crowd's interests.

When you get on stage, you want to make sure that you have the best speech possible. Polishing that speech is an important piece of that. Do not skip this step.

Chapter 21: Try Again

"Our greatest weakness lies in giving up. The most certain way to succeed is always to try just one more time."
— Thomas A. Edison

We all fail at times. If you have ever tried at anything in your life, you have been met with some sort of failure, regardless of whether it was big or small. The ability to get up and try once again is something that is intrinsic to any sort of success. Failing is just a part of any learning process, and learning to view it in such a light will help you tremendously in any future endeavor. If anything, you should begin to view failure as the catalyst for betterment. Instead of feeling defeated by a failure, it should propel you to try once more, or as many times as necessary, until you reach success.

Now, of course there are ways around failure, and we discuss many of them in this chapter. Having a clear-cut agenda or "plan" is essential for setting yourself up for success. Without a plan, it's far easier to be sidetracked.

Practicing is also key, because it also is a large component of success. Very few people, if any, are born "great" at something. The real masters are the ones that have committed to practice, in order to better themselves. Having your own form of a "guinea pig," by collecting a place or group of people to practice on and with, will help you improve. We learn from feedback, and this is essential for becoming more skilled. Creating structures that you will follow and work by is necessary, as well. Structure goes hand-in-hand with your agenda, but it is more detailed and more thought out. However, be aware of change and create structures that can be flexible when needed. They should be strong and well researched, but also malleable in case of crises.

However, even the most skilled people will be met with defeat, and this is where "trying again" comes into play.

If you do find yourself failing, these are a few things to consider:

- Assess your plan, and look for any weak links or points that may have aided in failure.

- Ask for feedback from the people that you have practiced with. Be open to criticism.

- Re-work the structures that you have created once more.

- Realize that failure is a part of life, and that you will grow from it.

Do not allow defeat to stop you from trying once more. True strength of character is being able to accept failure, brushing it aside, reevaluating your tactics, and trying once more. You will be surprised in your findings, and sometimes taking a second look at your plans will allow you to see far more clearly. Practice taking in "the bigger picture," so to speak, in order to see from point A to point B. However, do not overlook the details — they are just as important, but never lose sight of your end goal.

Trying is challenging, but, as we know, Rome wasn't built in a day. With implementing the above tactics, not losing faith in your goals, and careful planning and practice, you'll be able to build your own Rome in no time.

PART IV

Exuding Confidence

Chapter 22: Dress for Success

"Your appearance is your expression to others about who you are and what you stand for. The way you look reflects your self-image, attitude, confidence, and state of mind. A strong, purposeful presence is the hallmark of an effective image."
— Natalie Jobity

D o you notice a difference between when you wake up in your bedclothes and when you dress up for work? You may take a moment to look in the mirror and smile at yourself, and that's okay. You want to feel good about yourself. Feeling good gives you confidence, and that confidence will not only be visible from the way you're dressed, but also in the way you carry yourself because of the way you are dressed. If you're in a nice suit or dress, whichever you prefer wearing, you'll find yourself standing straighter, walking with purpose, and smiling more often.

Foremost, smiling is key. It shows that you're confident, and that confidence spreads when you smile. As the saying goes, smiles are contagious. There is a reason people say "dress for success." Dressing in nicer clothes imitates what you think of in terms of success, and when you begin to look successful, people start treating you that way. Dressing for success is more of a mindset that leads you to success. Of course, it's not all about the clothes, but when you look good, your charisma rises. And what do great leaders have? Charisma. You want to dress for success in order to develop your executive presence.

You've probably heard the phrase, "Don't judge a book by its cover." Though it's a nice sentiment, and maybe a good idea to put into practice, most people still judge the cover anyway. You must take that into account when you dress for success. People are going to judge your cover, and, if you're wearing jeans and a hoodie, what does that say about you? You want to come off as professional in every aspect that you can. The way you dress sets an example for your employees and impresses your clients. If your client sees the effort you've put into your appearance, he or she will know that you mean business.

When should you dress for success, you ask? All the time!

- Regular work hours

- Business meetings

- Business trips

- Charity events

- Social parties

- Interviews

There are probably a dozen different instances where it would benefit you to dress up, but these are the most important. Some businesspeople even dress for success on their personal vacations.

How much is too much? You have your suit or dress, your favorite pair of business shoes, and maybe even some jewelry, but when do your accessories go overboard? It is wise to keep jewelry simple because flashy displays could be distracting. Though tattoos are slowly becoming more acceptable in the Western workplace, you will want to cover up any that would misrepresent you or your company. Also, try to keep over-the-top patterns out of your wardrobe. That neon green, zebra print tie might have been a hit at a party, but not so much at your workplace. All in all, keep it simple, with maybe one item that accents your business style.

These days, you no longer have to spend a fortune to dress for success. As more and more people dress up for work, many affordable, stylish clothing lines have entered the picture. You no longer have to spend two hundred dollars on one suit. Shopping smart will allow you to purchase multiple articles of clothing that are appropriate for the workplace for less. That's something we all want to hear.

You want to dress for success because:

- It makes you feel good, which boosts confidence.

- Increased self-image leads to mental health benefits.

- Your employees and clients will be impressed.

- The way you carry yourself will command respect.

- It reflects your company's image.

Remember, each company is different, and how you dress depends on the message you want your company to send. If you're in the fashion industry, wearing what's considered "in style" will reflect more than the standard business suit. If you work with children, dressing a little more casual could be more appropriate. Evaluate what professionals in your industry wear, and then make an informed decision. You want to stand out, not stick out.

Chapter 23: Be Confident, Not Arrogant

"Believe in yourself! Have faith in your abilities!
Without a humble but reasonable confidence in your
own powers you cannot be successful or happy."
— **Norman Vincent Peale**

I t is perfectly natural to want to walk into a room filled with people and make a good impression. For many people, however, the feat of actually walking into a crowded room and making a splash is nerve-racking. You want people to think highly of you because gaining an audience's trust matters for your business. Because of television shows and movies, we now associate leaders with charisma — the elite of the elite, but being at the top of your game doesn't mean you should treat those around you differently.

When it comes to exuding confidence, it is best to be confident without coming across as arrogant. Why? Confidence is the result of believing in your abilities as a trusting individual, and that you can succeed in your goals. Confidence comes after you realize people can rely on you, and when other people know it, too. To be confident is to be self-assured in your own qualities because you have come to appreciate them about yourself.

Arrogance, however, occurs when you over-value your importance when it is not deserved. It leaves no room for humility and loses peoples' respect.

There are many strategies available for you to use to leave behind the impression you want to carry over to people. Ranging from the way you present yourself to how you mentally prepare yourself, you can bring confidence into a room and leave arrogance out of the way. By doing so, you will conduct yourself with executive presence. Great leaders achieve a much needed balance where they respect themselves and those around them, and the people they meet respect them in turn.

First, critically think about the way you present yourself. People gravitate to individuals they think are approachable and sincere. People can recognize someone who walks into a room and considers him or herself a big shot, and it turns them off. Instead, when you introduce yourself, use an inviting smile, maintain a positive attitude, stay relaxed, and (when possible) work to engage those around you in meaningful conversation.

Once you strike up a conversation, practice your listening skills by asking questions so you can get to know the person better — and so you can start to build a relationship with him or her. Perhaps chit-chatting with a stranger makes you nervous. If so, own this knowledge about yourself and use it get past this obstacle. We often feel more confident in our own abilities when we do not focus on ourselves but on another person. Tell yourself that you are here to help this person with your skills and services, and then make the conversation about them and what they need! You will get out of your own way, and you will demonstrate your abilities and care for the person at the same time.

You may think of yourself as skilled in the art of talking versus the art of listening. If this describes you, give yourself a new rule: do not dominate a conversation. Yes, you want to share about yourself and what you can offer, but you want to take turns talking. A conversation should not be a one-sided version of your greatest hits, but a chance to build a relationship. If you notice you are overriding the other person, ask a question and take a turn in the role of the listener. This way you give others a chance to engage in this moment with you, and you can determine when to offer your opinion again. By taking turns, you will show you are confident in your ability to speak without coming across as stuck up because you will illustrate to others that you value what they have to say.

In order to make the impression that you are confident rather than arrogant, keep in mind that you can influence how other people perceive you. One of the best things you can do is to stay engaged in the moment. An arrogant person will act as though they have a better place to be than with the person or people they are with at the moment. Don't do this. Instead, think of the opportunity to be around people — whether it's at the water cooler, your conference room, or a stage — as a gift, because people are giving you their time by being there. Act grateful. Even though you are busy and have a million other things to do, keep yourself in the moment. This is where you belong. Be confident in that.

You will not excel at presenting yourself every time. You will make small mistakes. Maybe you need to rush to a meeting and are abrupt with your employee or co-worker. Maybe you forget to turn your cell phone off while meeting with a customer and the ringer goes off. Or better yet, it is possible that while watching a video of yourself giving a speech, you described what you do with too many over exaggerated statements. You are human, and humans make mistakes. The true test is to own those mishaps. Apologize where you can and learn from each circumstance so you can do better next time.

Not every interaction is going to be perfect, and that's okay. Do your best to build relationships, but also understand that sometimes it may be out of your control. You cannot force people to like you. Thank the person for their time, pat yourself on the back for doing your best anyway, and keep going. An arrogant attitude tells you that you are above self-improvement, but you know better. Finding and using an attitude of confidence will help you to fare well in the long run.

In order to feel confident, you must trust in your abilities and in your ability to learn. In order to project confidence, you must value yourself and treat people with the proper value and respect that they, in turn, deserve. With the correct attitude, you will thrive in your interactions with others.

Chapter 24: Kindness and Confidence

"Kindness in words creates confidence. Kindness in thinking creates profoundness. Kindness in giving creates love."
—Lao Tzu

We have all had those days where we are stuck on a project and feel down because of it. The project at work is taking much longer than we first thought it would. And because of this, we're lacking in confidence. Or how about the day when you received feedback from your boss about the last project he or she thinks you did not do a great job on? You probably were not feeling the best about yourself at that moment. You felt like you lacked a certain drive to continue. Maybe you even thought that what you were good at now seems like the opposite.

The good news is you are not alone. It might feel like you are, but you are not. Now repeat that to yourself a couple times over. You need to remember this! Even though your self-esteem meter is low in this moment, it does not mean you should give up on what you have been done or are doing.

Most likely, you missed the words of reassurance your boss gave you after he or she told you that your last project was not your best work. These words of reassurance are easily missed especially after you have been hit with bad news. What is within these words from your boss is something you should not miss: kindness.

Your boss shared those kind words of reassurance with you to build up your confidence. You are not always going to successfully complete a project. There will be obstacles and challenges along the way that you will need to face. Again, you are not alone in this. Your boss is building your confidence for a reason. He or she knows you can take the project on and successfully complete it this time around.

This is not only limited to unsuccessfully finishing a project. This scenario is but one of the many you may find yourself in. It could be missing an important deadline, losing a customer, or upsetting a co-worker. Whatever it may be, there is always hope and words of kindness waiting for you. Honestly, nothing feels better. When you are feeling down about yourself and your potential, a few words of reassurance can turn your whole day around. You will find yourself trying that much harder the next chance you get. You are learning from your mistakes and gaining confidence in the process.

You want to know the best part about this? You can take this experience and share it with someone else. Not only are you passing kind words along to someone else, but you are also providing someone with a tangible experience to learn from as well. Words of kindness go a long way, when you think about it. Confidence comes soon after. However, this is not an immediate building of it. This takes dedicated time and many attempts at practice. Soon your confidence will continue to build, but remember to not let it get the best of you.

Chapter 25: Build a Relationship with Your Audience

"You can make more friends in two months by becoming interested in other people than you can in two years by trying to get other people interested in you."
—Dale Carnegie

Nothing will make you feel more confident than talking to someone you know. Building a relationship with your audience puts your mind at ease because you have established mutual trust and respect. Friendliness is key to building the relationship. When you arrive in the presentation room, or send that email, you have to consider your audience. Your audience will determine the tone and attitude you have when speaking to him, her, or them. However, no matter who your audience is, there are two things you should always be: polite and friendly.

Let's begin by talking about your first type of audience, the people whom you are meeting for the first time. You might not know a lot about him or her, other than the fact he or she is new. Therefore, before you enter the meeting or send the email, do your own research.

Learn as many characteristics about your audience as possible:

- Demographics & psychographics (age, race, gender, education level, origin, preferences, etc.)

- Expectations

- How much your audience knows about what you will discuss

To build a relationship with someone new, don't just jump right into business. Ask your client or employee how he or she is and say you're pleased to meet him or her. Be friendly from the start and use their names a lot to create a comfortable atmosphere. Pay attention to your body language, so that you appear as open as possible. Once you've established a friendly atmosphere, you can talk business, but building the relationship doesn't end there. You must continue to personalize that information and make eye contact, so that your audience knows you care and are willing to listen. Open the table to ideas and suggestions, so your client or employee understands his or her input matters.

When presenting to or emailing someone that you have already begun to build a relationship with, make sure you maintain that relationship. Similarly, when you first walk into the room, or open the email, ask how your audience is doing. This time, however, if you've already established a relationship, you should mention something more specific so he or she knows you are genuinely interested in his or her life and well-being. Again, pay attention to your body language and voice. You want to switch up your vocals so you can emphasize your points differently.

Here are some tricks to build a relationship in face-to-face meetings:

- Greet your audience.

- Smile often.

- Maintain eye contact.

- Shake everyone's hand.

- Keep a straight and alert posture.

- Use hand gestures when speaking.

- Use everyone's names (first or last, depending on how well you already know them) to personalize the meeting.

- Ask your audience's opinions.

- Close on a friendly, positive note and thank everyone for coming.

Building a relationship is a little different through email but, when carefully treated, it can be just as effective. After all, if couples can maintain long-distance relationships online, business relationships can succeed, too.

Here are some tips for building relationships through email:

- Begin with a friendly hello, asking how he or she is doing.

- Be sure to write his or her name throughout the email to ensure that personal touch.

- Recall topics that he or she likes, and suggest tasks or ideas that would suit him or her based on what you've observed.

- Ask for his or her opinion about an idea or multiple ideas you proposed in the email.

- Say you look forward to hearing from him or her soon.

- Keep in frequent contact.

- Respond to emails as soon as possible.

Of course, another thing to keep in mind is the size of your audience. It is much easier to personalize a meeting or an email when there is one person, or only a few people. You can still somewhat personalize your message to a larger audience based on region, education level, etc., but some things, like addressing people by name or shaking hands, will have to be left out. That doesn't necessarily mean you can't connect to larger audiences, but it requires more preparation and work.

With larger audiences, starting with an anecdote that everyone can relate to will often hook them. However, it is essential that you understand who is in your audience before you jump into a story because, if you start talking about something they can't relate to, you'll lose them.

If you use these simple tips, you will find that people are more receptive to what you have to say and are looking forward to meetings with you. As long as you are friendly and polite, building relationships will be a breeze.

Chapter 26: Answering Audience's Questions

"Confidence, like art, never comes from having all the answers; it comes from being open to all the questions."
—Earl Gray Stevens

Some questions are easy to answer: how was your weekend? Can I get you some water? Was that movie any good? Other questions are a little harder. When you have an audience waiting on a fast answer, there's a lot of pressure. But if you stay calm and confident, you can handle any question they throw at you.

It's not necessary to open the floor for questions, but, if you do, people are going to feel more valued and connected, so it's worth trying. Some questions will be easy to address — asking for clarifications, elaborations, and specifications is common. Other things are more complicated. If you know the answer to something, it's important to give it, even if it's unpleasant. You want to be trustworthy. If you don't know an answer, admit it. That can be hard, but, again, it builds trust. It also humanizes you, and you can always offer to find the requested information for the future. No one respects a presenter who hems and haws and avoids the question.

Answering questions sounds simple, and it can be. We all have plenty of experience.

If you really want to excel, there are a few things you can do to take your answers to the next level.

- Think ahead. What kinds of questions can you expect? Practice answering them.

- Announce that you'll be taking questions, or your audience may be afraid to speak up.

- Often, no one wants to ask the first question. Consider asking an audience member you know — a friend or colleague — to ask an opening question. Once the ball is rolling, others will be more comfortable participating.

- Provide paper so people can write down questions.

- Have paper for yourself to write down questions you can't answer. Later, you can find the information for next time.

- Don't let questioners ramble.

- Don't interrupt questioners who aren't rambling.

- Don't assume you know what's being asked without taking time to listen to the whole question. Pay attention.

- Don't rush into things. Take a moment to think about your answer.

- Repeat the question so that the entire audience can hear.

- Ask for the name of the questioner.

- Address everyone when answering. Begin and end your response with the questioner, but don't let it become a conversation between the two of you.

- Check with the questioner. Make sure your answer was understood.

- Don't get into arguments with your audience.

- Be confident.

- Be honest.

- Speak well — make sure the audience can hear and understand you.

- Be clear and concise.

- Maintain confident and interested body language.

- If questions are extremely specific or complex, and will bore or go over the heads of most of your audience, offer to talk privately to the questioner later. Have a one-on-one conversation and avoid making your audience sit through something unnecessary and uninteresting for them.

Be confident, honest, and approachable, and you can handle answering any question asked of you.

Chapter 27: Be Present, In Your Own Skin

*"No one else can make you feel inferior
without your consent."*
—Eleanor Roosevelt

There is only one you in the entire world. There may be similar people, but remember they aren't exactly like you. Even identical twins have slight differences. Embrace you, because, until you do, your presence in a room will not matter. You want to matter, because guess what? Your message, whatever that may be, is important to the world. Only you can accomplish what you were meant to accomplish, so take a step back and reflect on how gifted you are.

- Brainstorm. Make a list of your strengths. Remember moments of success and determine what you did to bring that success about. You may be tempted to reflect on shortcomings as well, but resist the urge.

- Ask for feedback. Talk with a trusted friend or advisor about the things you do well. An outside perspective might be exactly what you need to see yourself in a positive light.
- Test yourself. There are numerous assessments online that help you to determine what your strengths are.

After you start to become comfortable with yourself and find your inner peace, you can take note of how you are present in other aspects of your life. Think about driving home at night from work. Are you checked in when driving, or has it become so routine that you forget how you ended up back at home? Just like how you should not check out while driving, you should never check out when you are talking to those people who matter in your world. Keep in mind: everyone matters.

Always stay focused and be on point in every aspect of your life to be present in your own skin. Put the cell phone, your to-do list, or that speech you're writing away, and focus on the now. Keep your mind in check when talking to the person in front of you, or when working on a task.

You may find there are certain techniques that help you focus. Some people play with their pen, or chew gum, to focus their thoughts. While this is useful to you, it may not appear professional to others. Find ways of focusing that are both useful and appropriate.

- Take notes. You may find it helps you focus on the topic at hand if you write it down.

- Be involved. To remain engaged in the moment, use those excellent listening skills you've been practicing. When you need clarification, ask for it. If you have an idea, suggest it (at an appropriate time).

Remaining present and actively engaged in your surroundings is essential. You'll be surprised how much more productive and successful you are, in all aspects of your life, if you just follow that simple rule.

Chapter 28: Be Confident in Your Abilities

"We gain strength, and courage, and confidence by each experience in which we really stop to look fear in the face...we must do that which we think we cannot."
—Eleanor Roosevelt

Have you ever heard the phrase, "fake it 'til you make it"? It's one of those marvelous phrases that rings true for almost every aspect of your life. When you act confident, eventually you will become confident. It sounds easy, right? But it really isn't if you think about all of the obstacles you are faced with every day. However, it's definitely achievable with a positive attitude, clear thinking and planning, and modest acting ability.

It's been proven that dressing the part automatically increases a person's self-worth. Think about it: a new outfit, a new tie — you always feel a little better after putting it on. It may not boost your confidence level sky-high, but it's a factor in your general outlook on the day.

However, learning to manage your newfound confidence comes with its own set of rules. There is a fine line between being confident and being arrogant, but if you break them down, they're really not so hard to distinguish between. A confident person is comfortable in his or her own skin, open to communication, and able to articulate opinions clearly and respectfully. An arrogant person attempts to take up the entire room, belittles others in communication, and refuses to listen to others' opinions. Do you see the difference?

In order to be confident, you must first believe in yourself and your ideas. You should allow for varying opinions, but not let criticism sway you from your points.

So, in order to be successfully confident, there are a few things that you must remember:

- Dress the part. Even if the event you are attending isn't necessarily formal, take time to make sure that you are presentable and appropriate. Taking care of yourself will automatically boost your self-respect, as well as make others respect you, too.

- Practice being comfortable in your own skin. This is incredibly important, because people who are happy with themselves are oftentimes magnetic to others. People want to be around happy people. Make a mental (or physical) list of your best attributes and remember to review these often. This sort of review will also aid you in difficult situations.

- Never show defeat or uncertainty, but instead, exude the appearance of being in control (even when you feel as if you are not). Also, have faith in your abilities, and work on realizing that you are just as capable as anyone in the room. Don't take rejection to heart, but instead, learn to accept it while still maintaining your confidence.

Be careful to not overstep your boundaries, and periodically check to make sure that you are not acting in a way that could be considered arrogant.

You can monitor yourself by watching for these specific things:

- Be kind to everyone. Respect others, so that they will respect you.

- Be open to communication of all forms, and make a point to listen to everyone, regardless of your personal feelings and whether or not you agree with them.

- Invite everyone into the conversation, and strive to form relationships that aren't just surface-level. Make a real attempt to connect with your audience.

- Lastly, don't scorn or refuse to answer questions, regardless of what they might be. Make a point to answer any question in the best of your ability. This shows that you respect the question and the person.

Confidence is completely psychological, and it can be learned. While others are born more confident than some, this mindset is achievable through realizing your strengths, acting the part, taking care of yourself and others, and respecting both yourself and the people around you.

PART V

Commanding Authority

Chapter 29: Stepping Up

"When placed in command, take charge."
—Norman Schwarzkopf

When you're in a position of leadership, you can't be passive. You need to take charge and step up. Previous chapters mentioned how being friendly is great for building relationships, but you also need to stand firm. You can't let things slide by because you don't want to look like the bad guy. You must be decisive, and sometimes you have to act quickly without much time to second-guess yourself.

To command authority, you need to set standards for yourself. Do you want to be known for being efficient, on top of projects, and in control? Then you need to take a moment, believe in your own abilities, and assume that air of authority. You can do it. You are a leader. So you've created a positive work environment and everyone is excited to work, but now you have to show everyone who's the boss. You can still be a great boss and command authority. When something needs to be done, and done fast, you need to voice your thoughts. Let your employees know what you want done and when you want it finished.

Here are some ways you can step up and effectively lead without being off-putting:

- Examine your projects and think of the ultimate goal of each. Which is more important?

- Prioritize: know which projects need to be done immediately and communicate this to your employees.

- Don't waver: make sure your voice (in person and in emails) shows certainty.

- Give positive feedback to employees who complete projects on time, so they are encouraged, but make sure that when projects are turned in late you communicate with the employee(s) responsible and let them know that late projects are unacceptable (repeats could have negative consequences).

- Explain the projects as thoroughly as possible and answer questions to avoid miscommunication.

- Set dates for each project to be completed by and make it clear that these dates are non-negotiable.

- Keep tabs on everyone and ask how their projects are coming along (if your employees know you're going to come around asking, they're going to make sure they have something done to show they've been working).

- Be straightforward and honest: if you're happy with a project, let your employees know and, likewise, if you're disappointed with something, make it clear and describe what you dislike about the work.

Sometimes mistakes happen. Miscommunication, misinterpretation, or a lack of direction can steer a project off the path. You need to remain calm, explain more clearly, and talk to your employees so you know they understand what they're doing. Don't "forget about" the flops, either. Learn from them and use them as examples on how not to do something. If one approach didn't work, reflect on why and then try a different approach. As long as you keep your cool, you can even turn flops around and put them back on track.

When your employees see that you're still standing straight and speaking with calm assertiveness, they will be confident they've put they're trust in the right person. You will be their motivation. If they think you're supporting and leading them in the right direction, they will complete each task the way you wanted it, and, hopefully, with enthusiasm because you stepped up and commanded authority.

Chapter 30: True Leadership

"The most dangerous leadership myth is that leaders are born — that there is a genetic factor to leadership. That's nonsense; in fact, the opposite is true. Leaders are made rather than born."
—Warren Bennis

True leadership occurs when someone can successfully guide and direct a group of people or an organization. So, how do you recognize true leadership when you see it? As a leader in your business, how do you exemplify true leadership?

You may be lucky. Perhaps you have had past managers or mentors that immediately spring to mind who you associate with true leadership. These individuals will be great examples to model your own behavior after. On the other hand, you may not immediately think of someone you personally know, and that's okay. More than likely, you still have an idea of how a true leader should conduct him or herself while in business. This is a starting place you can draw from as you begin to think about how you can show true leadership.

When it comes to true leadership, we commonly think of the following characteristics:

- Inspirational: this person has a vision and the ability to convince others to follow it. He makes the people around him feel valued and instrumental in achieving his vision. He not only shares his vision, but also makes others excited to support it while he inspires them to believe they can achieve their own, too.

- Driven: this person believes goals are achievable. She knows how to set up a sequence of actions to reach small goals to obtain larger ones. She understands how to use her own talents and abilities to reach her goals, and how other peoples' talents and abilities can play a part in this process as well.

- Organized: this person knows how to designate time, resources, and personal energy to keep a business running and moving towards its goals. He is able to project confidence because he is not rushing into a meeting unprepared. He takes care of himself and those around him so everyone can act on their full potential.

- Ready: this person is capable of making decisions for the good of everyone as soon as it is needed. She projects confidence in her ability to direct a business, knows when to step in and make the decisions herself, and when a decision can be made by someone else. She does not need to force people to follow her lead with inappropriate tactics because she has learned how to communicate with people to motivate them.

- Respectful: this person, even though he is a leader, remains humble. He recognizes the value of other peoples' work and ideas in connection to his own, and he openly communicates this sentiment to them. He considers how his business and services can positively impact the lives of those around him.

- Honest: this person follows her principles and deserves others' trust. She does not employ dishonest tactics in her business. She follows the same standards she expects others to follow, and her employees and customers feel they are treated fairly by her business.

Of course, the list above gives examples of traits found in true leaders that we often think about or find admirable. It's meant to get you thinking, but it's not all-inclusive.

Now, it's your turn. In order to act as a true leader, you must first identify what you consider leadership to be before you can discern it in others and, more importantly, in yourself. We all possess an individual understanding of what leadership means to us, ranging from guiding a group of people, to directing an office, to inspiring a team of people to act. What do you consider the marks of a true leader? Take out a piece of paper, give yourself two minutes on the clock, and write down a list of characteristics.

Now, take a good look at your list. Go through and circle any descriptors you want to possess as a true leader. Then pick two to three characteristics you want to work on so you can build up your true leadership skills. Take each characteristic you starred, put ten minutes on the clock, and brainstorm three specific ways you can act out this characteristic in your organization. Put your plan into action and note how your interactions improve with people after a month, after two months, and so on. Once you consciously decide how you want to conduct yourself as a leader, you will be able to measure your own leadership skills and take that knowledge to better yourself.

It may seem daunting to be a leader to someone else when you first think of all the ways you can improve yourself, but you are capable. You do not need to build the mountain. Instead, think of the trait you want to exemplify as a stone. Once you improve on that one stone, it is in your pile and you are ready to work on the next stone to add on top of it. Soon, you have perfected your base, then you have a hill, and, before you know it, you have built the mountain. Remember, you can work on any characteristic you choose to be the true leader you want to be by consciously acting it out in your day-to-day life.

Chapter 31: When to Shout

*"We can't change the world by shouting, but our words
can have meaning if we give them enough respect."*
—Evan Meekins

W hat do you think of when you think of the word "shout"? Do
you think of fans at a sporting event or two people arguing over
a misunderstanding? Well, both are correct in the sense that
people are raising their voices to get their point across. What about in the
work place? Well, this is where it gets a bit trickier.

The word "shout" does not carry a positive connotation with it. Because of
this, it is probably not something you want to do within the work area, right?
The answer to this is yes and no. Different people have different ways of using
authority. Some may find that shouting is the only way his or her employees
will listen. The amount of respect for this boss, however, is debatable.

Imagine the last time you were yelled at. You probably were not excited
about the fact someone was yelling at you. This did not make you feel good

about yourself either. Why is this? When someone raises his or her tone of voice or even his or her volume, we are taken aback by it. This usually signals that something is wrong or something did not go as planned. Frustration is let loose when an individual shouts. However, this is not the only way. There are other ways to use one's authority.

Immediacy is another pathway to take to show authority. This lets another worker know when something is urgent or of utmost importance without barging into an individual's comfort zone by shouting. Alarm might still be instilled into the individual but not to the extreme that shouting brings.

If you want to create a respectable executive presence, this is the pathway to take. Raising your voice at a worker will only make him or her lose respect for you. This is the last thing you want to happen in your line of work—whatever it might be! Many times people think of an iron fist when they think of authority. This is not how it has to be. By finding a more respectable way of showing your authority, you will soon see a more relaxed atmosphere for both yourself and employees.

This relaxed atmosphere brings many benefits. Workers will find themselves more comfortable approaching you with issues they may be having with their work, another employee, or even in their personal lives outside of work. When you show respect to people, they will most likely return that respect to you. Therefore, your workers will show respect to your authority as long as you respect them as individuals and as a team.

At some point, you were probably in the position your workers are in. You might have experienced what it was like to be shown authority in a discouraging way. Think back to how that made you feel. Instead of repeating that for your workers, find a better, more respectful way of going about it.

Chapter 32: When to Apologize

"Never ruin an apology with an excuse."
—Benjamin Franklin

We all make mistakes sometimes. In business, it's important to learn when to apologize and accept the fact that you did something wrong. It is not an easy task to manage, but it's one that can set you free to become more relatable to your clients, your employees, your superiors, and even your family. Becoming a better authority figure involves this simple step. The difficult part is discovering when to apologize and when not to.

First off, realize it's absolutely okay to apologize. We are all human. Not a single one of us is infallible. You will make mistakes, and, in business, you may make really huge mistakes. This is where you place your ego at the door and realize that it is absolutely going to happen. It happens to everyone. People go through life making mistakes everyday.

There are times when you should apologize and take steps to make that apology sincere in the business world.

Ask yourself the following questions to make sure you are apologizing for the right reasons:

- Who is the apology to? Is the apology going to be for you or is it going to be for the other person? Make sure you are sincere and believe that the apology is honestly for something that you did wrong. Reflect on the wrong and come up with the correct apology.

- What is the apology for? Maybe you missed a deadline and the customer is unhappy. They relied on you to have your work done when it needed to be and you did not have it completed. You underestimated the time it took to complete the work. Just be honest, and explain the situation to them.

- How do you make the apology? For decisions on how to make the apology, it depends on context. How close of a person was this to you? Were they an important client that you've been working with for years? A new prospect? If possible, of course, a sincere in-person apology is best. However, sometimes making an in-person apology isn't a possibility. The next best option is via phone, and the last would be email. Forming a sincere email apology takes work, but it's possible.

Again, before making the apology, spend some time reflecting on what it was you did wrong. It could be just a simple error or a big one. Either way, reflecting on the error can make you a better person and help build a better business. Learning about what you did wrong can help you to never make that error again, which makes it easier to help out clients or yourself in the future.

Most importantly in this process, have humility. Truly feel sorry for the wrong you have committed to this person. If you try and apologize without being humble, it will show you are not sincere. This will only hurt you. The person you are apologizing to will eventually let it go. Word of you being insincere can get around and can tarnish your reputation. You want to make sure that does not happen. A big part of learning in business and life is to accept when you make mistakes, learn, and grow from them.

Chapter 33: Learning from Your Team

"I must follow the people. Am I not their leader?"
—Benjamin Disraeli

Without someone to lead, a leader is nothing. You need other people, and, if you work closely with them, you'll be surprised by what you can learn. Be open to unexpected lessons, and cultivate strong relationships with the people you work with. No one likes a dictator, and you have a much better chance at implementing change if you're willing to undergo some change together. People are social creatures, and you need your team just as much as they need you.

When you're used to being in charge, it can be hard to step back and let yourself learn from others. Put in the effort. If you learn how and when to follow, your leadership will improve. It will build community and strengthen your bond with your followers. You can't lead effectively without communication and collaboration.

Have you ever made an insightful comment in a class or meeting, surprising a supervisor who'd never thought of that point before? Do you remember the pride and exhilaration it left you with? You have the opportunity to make your team feel like that every day. All leaders have to start somewhere and, by listening to others and taking them seriously, you can help them get that start. Everyone always has something to learn. Let yourself be taught.

It all starts with communication — specifically listening. You've already read the chapter on listening, so let's talk about what comes next.

- Pay attention. Watch your team working. Watch them interacting. Take notes, mentally and physically on how you can improve in your interaction with them.

- Always take into account any contributions to the conversation.

- Learn more about your team. Who's good at what? If they have a skill that could be even better, help them grow it.

- Don't hesitate to seek out help and advice. If you've achieved the previous step, you should know who can help in different areas.

- Know what people want. Know what they need. Let them point you in the right direction, and lead them from there. If you're too focused on being in charge, you're going to miss something important.

- Don't underestimate people. They may know their limits better than you do.

- You're a human leader, not a sheepdog. Encourage people to think for themselves and take the initiative. You never know when another leader could be born from stepping back.

- Welcome polite conflict. You're not always right.

- Stay calm. Make sure that polite conflict remains polite, and keep it contained to appropriate times and places.

- Make sure your team understands that they're a part of this. Let them know they're valued.

- Understand that no matter what position you're in, you are a part of a team. Trust them. Rely on them. Sometimes you might have to let go and let someone else take the lead, and that's okay. You should all be there for each other.

Stepping back and opening up is hard, but it's worth it. Let yourself be a follower sometimes, too. You're not more important than the people you're leading. You just have a different position and skill set. Focus on the people, not on the leadership itself, and you'll learn amazing things.

Chapter 34: Listening to Your Team

"It takes a great man to be a good listener."
—Calvin Coolidge

N o man can walk alone. We need our team of people to hold us accountable and to grow a strong business. As the leader of your team, it's necessary to actually spend time listening to the needs of your team rather than being the opposing force ignoring what they truly want. A great team player and strong leader spends time understanding his or her staff and doing what he or she can to help them succeed.

When building a business, your team wants to feel like they are important to you. They are important to you, because without their help you cannot succeed in anything. Those are the facts. I'm certain, since you picked up this book, that you want to succeed in building a business that will grow immensely. You want to be successful. Being a great listener will help that.

Most people listen only enough to have a response. That is not active listening, but rather putting yourself in front of the person you are talking to and showing that you do not care about them. If you know that you are a poor listener, there are ways to combat that and develop skills to become a better listener.

Here is a list of ways to show your team that you care:

- Take notes. If you know that you have trouble listening, make it a point to take notes about what the person is saying. Listen as he or she talks and write down what you find is important, or the key thoughts that the person is saying. If you are worried about the person questioning your motives for taking notes, make it about him or her. Communicate that what he or she has to say is so important that you don't want to forget anything talked about and you want to remember it later. If people are talking too fast, have them slow down, because remember, they matter, and if they know they are truly being listened to, they will be willing to help you with what you need.

- Avoid distractions. Having a cell phone out while talking to a person, having a television on, Facebook up, anything that could distract you from the person you are focused on, is not what you want to display. When you have these devices out, it shows the person you are talking to that whatever is on that phone, television, or computer has more value than him or her. Remember, you want to show people that they are valuable. Because they are.

- Ask questions. Nothing says you are listening more than asking questions to the person you are having the conversation with. If he or she brings up a point of interest, say, "Tell me more about that." Make sure to ask as many questions as possible. This also helps you to form solid decisions if it's something that is important for the company. Your team may have the exact ideas you need to fix a problem that you have been having. You never know unless you ask.

Bottom line: care about your team. Know what is happening with them and listen to what they have to say. It will make you a better leader and they will be better workers.

Chapter 35: Be the Leader They Need You To Be

"If your actions inspire others to dream more, learn more, do more and become more, you are a leader."
—John Quincy Adams

Becoming a leader is a challenging, as well as rewarding, job. Not only are you responsible for the people under you, but you are also expected to face, head-first, any and all of the problems that will inevitably come your way at some point during your career. To lead is to have faith in yourself, in your team, and to be able to recognize the right decisions. Leading is not about being at "the top," but it is about managing and taking care of your followers, weathering any storm, and maintaining focus and direction.

For a true leader, there are a few things that you must have under your belt in order to succeed. Let's break these down now:

- Confidence: to excel in your leadership role, having the confidence to do so is key. This kind of confidence takes many forms. You will need the confidence to "dream big" but also realize and address any dangers or consequences. You will also need to maintain faith in yourself and your team when up against failure and rejection. This is something that comes from within, and is helped by a clear focus, attention to detail, and strategic planning.

- Speaking your mind, respectfully: sometimes it's necessary to play "bad cop" in a scenario. You will be faced with difficult people, and being able to defend yourself, your opinions, and your goals is incredibly important. However, you should practice doing so in a respectful manner. No one likes the hotheaded guy in the room, who can fly off the handle at any moment. Learn to channel your frustration, directing it in a way that is positive, yet stern. It is necessary to command, but do so gently. The kind leader is a leader who is loved.

- Listen: being a good listener is just as important as being a good communicator. Listen to your team, and value their opinions. Do not let your leadership role go to your head, but instead, realize that to lead, you must also learn. Remember that you chose the people on your team for a reason, and their thoughts and ideas are just as important as your own. Make it known that you are more than willing to take suggestions, and that you welcome them. Though you are the leader, your team should run like a democracy.

There's a reason there are so few good leaders. It's a challenging role, certainly, and people can oftentimes get caught up in their power. While it's necessary to have self-respect, it's also equally as necessary to respect those who are under you. In essence, you are taking care of these people, and your number one goal should be leading them in the right path, and looking out for both of your interests, collectively. You could not function without them, and vice versa.

This also means that you will be the one who shoulders the heaviest loads. It will be you who deals with the major problems that might arise, and it will also be you who accepts blame. This should not frighten you, but instead fill you with a sense of pride and purpose. These people have put their faith in you — YOU! That is such an incredible thing to experience, and it is one that you should cherish.

Be the leader you would want to follow, and, in time, you will become that leader — the leader your team needs you to be. Take a moment and list the characteristics that you admire in your role models and past leaders — such as presidents and other public figures. Study these peoples' lives, and implement their positive characteristics into your own life and leadership. We can always look to the past for inspiration, and doing so will help you to shape your own trademark leadership style.

PART VI

Owning the Room

Chapter 36: Scouting Out the Room

*"Accuracy of observation is the equivalent
of accuracy of thinking."*
—Wallace Stevens

W hen you walk into the room where you will deliver your presentation, there is an important step to complete. Before you even smile and wave, before you introduce yourself, you need to scout out the room. Take a close look at your audience and determine the kind of crowd you are presenting to. If you don't take the time to do that, you can't tailor your presentation and it won't be as great as it could have been.

Observing your audience is crucial to your presentation. How they're doing and what they're doing is going to affect how well they listen to you.

When scouting out the room, pay attention to:

- Alertness: pay attention to body language. Is everyone falling asleep because it's crash time? Are they full of energy because they just had their morning coffee?

- The overall mood: are they smiling from a recent successful project? Or sour because something went wrong?

- Potential distractions: this could be a flickering light, loud heater/AC, a squeaky chair, etc.

- The size of the room: is there space for you to move around the audience to grab their attention or will you have to remain at the front?

- What you have to work with: look for whiteboard, chalkboard, props, etc.

Let's take a closer look at some of these details. Why do you want your audience to be alert? Well, you want them to listen to you. That's why you're there. Alertness can help your presentation or ruin it. Too little alertness and your audience is hunching in their chairs, struggling to keep their eyes open, and not asking questions. Too much alertness and they're jittery, distracted by other sounds and what's happening outside the window. You want to make sure your audience has the right amount of alertness and, to do that, you need to stay engaging. Wake them up and/or snag their attention from the beginning of your presentation. Then actively speak to them to maintain that alertness throughout the presentation.

You also need to gather a sense of the overall room. You want to create positive energy for your presentation. If everyone in the room is already smiling and in a good mood from a recent success, because it's a nice day, or some other reason, then you have less work cut out for you. The positive energy is there and ready to be put to use in your presentation. If, however, there is low morale from a recent mistake, or if there is a general atmosphere of gloom, you will have to create that positive energy. Start your presentation with some happy thoughts, an anecdote, good news for the company, or another relevant topic to focus the positivity.

Potential distractions are presentation killers. Not only will distractions take away your audience's attention, they could also trip you up during your presentation. If there's a flickering light or a loud AC you can't speak over, you may want to consider moving the presentation to another room. If, however, you cannot move, you will just have to engage with your audience members more often than planned so they pay more attention to you. After all, they don't want to be caught off guard and not paying attention. Remember, the more distractions you have in the room, the more you will have to make your presentation interactive. If you've prepared for your presentation, and know your topics with minimal notes, adding more interaction shouldn't be difficult.

Check out the size of the room. If you have space to move around or through the audience (depending on how it's set up), you can walk around, and that adds more engagement instantly. Your audience will see you moving and focus on you to know where you're going and what you'll do next. If people are falling asleep, ask them questions, ask their opinion, and find a way to have them engage with one another briefly in order to bring back their alertness. Simply standing at the front of the room may not be as engaging but, if the room is a small size, your options may be limited. If you are stuck at the front, be sure to use hand gestures or draw diagrams related to your topic. Whatever it is you prefer to do, check to see if your audience is engaged and responding to your presentation.

Use whatever you have to work with in the room to make your presentation as interesting and engaging as possible. Sure, you have your PowerPoint, but also make use of any whiteboards, chalkboards, or props to emphasize a point you may think is especially important for your audience to know. Don't overdo it, or you'll lose your audience's attention by creating your own distractions. Pay attention to the audience. Their expressions and posture will often clue you in to what your next move should be.

Now that you know what to look for, analyze what you've found and incorporate it into your presentation. After your initial hellos, you should be able to launch into your topic with confidence. Own the room.

Chapter 37: Establishing Rapport

*"In many ways, effective communication begins
with mutual respect, communication that inspires,
and encourages others to do their best."*
—Zig Ziglar

Think of someone you know who you feel you have a strong bond with or feel at ease being around. How did this person build this relationship with you? Likely, this person reached out to you, found and expanded upon something you hold in common, and took time to learn what you consider important.

You build rapport with an audience when you focus on building a relationship with them. Typically, we think of charismatic or nurturing people as those who use rapport for social interactions. In order to have executive presence as a leader, so will you. The great news, however, is that, just like the other communication skills covered in this book, you can learn to use rapport in your interactions with others.

The first thing you should do before your event is research. Who is going to be in your audience? What ages will they be? Will they be mostly women or men? What do they want to learn from you? What does your audience likely already know when it comes to what you plan to talk about? How can they best relate to you and what you know? Take what you know about the people you will meet with and tailor your presentation the best that you can to match your expected audience. Just like in school, doing your homework will pay off — this knowledge establishes rapport because you can use it to connect with the people you plan to meet.

Another strategy is to arrive early to your own presentation, so you can introduce yourself to the people in the audience that you do not know. By being friendly and reaching out to people beforehand, you can get an earlier start on forging a connection with members of your audience. Better yet, any possible introductions to people in your audience will let you learn the names of a few people sitting out in the chairs during your talk. If it is suitable for your presentation and your presentation style, this means you can gesture to one of the people in the audience with his or her name, which will make your presentation more interactive and personable. Taking ten minutes to chitchat with people at your event will build your credibility as a friendly person (and — added bonus — should help reduce any anxiety you might feel). In the event that you cannot spend time with your audience beforehand, use a greeting in your introduction so your audience feels welcomed.

You can also establish rapport by the way you walk on to the stage or the way you take your place in the room, if it is a meeting. You should calmly enter the space and pleasantly smile at your audience before you begin your presentation. Since you already did your homework, emphasize what common ground you share with these people, or examples they can relate to, so your audience will see you as personable and approachable. To take this one step further, you can use inclusive language as you begin to near the end of your presentation, such as the word "we," instead of "I" or "me."

Use your time with these people to get a sense of their needs. This will help you build rapport because understanding their needs helps you to connect to them as people, and, when you show that you care about them, they connect to you. Make it clear to your audience that the skills and services you provide will help them achieve their goals.

Above all, when you enjoy what you do, people will connect to you. Teachers use rapport with students to great success by convincing their students that they enjoy their time with them. Likewise, you can build rapport with people during presentations, conference meetings, and one-on-one interactions, as long as you find pleasure in the opportunity to be with these people and the chance to better your relationships with them. Establishing rapport is a useful skill to have beyond the stage because it will improve your interactions with others across the board.

Chapter 38: The All-Important Introduction

"Never make a sales pitch as the way you introduce yourself. What you CAN say is how you help people and businesses."
—Beth Ramsay

When preparing a presentation, the introduction should be seen as one of the most important parts. Why would a short paragraph or first slide of a presentation be the most important? Well, your introduction is when the audience members decide whether they are interested in what you have to say about the topic at hand because your introduction prepares them for what you will say once you get going. If they're not interested, they might stand up and leave. If they are interested, you'll find them leaning forward in their seats. I'll let you decide which you would prefer.

Your goal is to captivate your audience. How you decide to go about this is completely up to you. Here are a few techniques to help you out:

• Introduce yourself. Even though the presentation may not be about you, your audience will wonder who you are and what you are doing in front of this group of people. Before you dive into the presentation, introduce yourself. Let them know your name and a little bit about you. This will help create a personal connection with your audience, instead of making it feel like a college lecture. Avoid spending too much time on yourself, though. Limit your information to a sentence or two and then jump into the introduction of the presentation.

- Make a first impression. You only have one chance to make an amazing first impression on your audience. You can always add more information to the body of your presentation when speaking, but your introduction is a one-time thing. Hook your audience with an interesting fact they may not have heard. A boring introduction will only lull your audience into a stupor. Statistics may be a great way to catch the attention of your audience. However, avoid using too many. Too many statistics will lose your audience members' attention and create a confusing introduction.

- Make this your road map. Your introduction should be organized and error free. It should be organized in the way that the rest of your presentation follows. If your first main point is your opinion on the topic, then the body of your presentation should cover that first. A short statement on how you came about the information, and the research you conducted, is a nice tidbit to add to your introduction. There should be no surprises waiting for your audience throughout your presentation. Your audience wants to know what you will be covering first and foremost. The rest of your presentation will then follow suit.

Always remember that your introduction makes the presentation either exciting and intriguing, or dull and disappointing. This sets the pace for your presentation. It might feel like there is a lot of pressure weighing down this small part of your presentation, but small parts of a whole can hold the most value for an audience member. Make the audience comfortable with your topic and then wow them with what you have to offer.

Chapter 39: Body Language

"The human body is the best picture of the human soul."
—Ludwig Wittgenstein

If you go into a project or situation with the mentality of defeat before you even begin, you do not stand a chance. The attitude you bring into your attempt to do something dramatically impacts your likelihood of success at it. In order to achieve success, you must project the belief that you can do it. You must train your mind to think you can not only accomplish the task before you, but also thrive as you do it.

We like to think that our minds influence our bodies, and not the other way around. In the past, people saw the relationship between mental decisions and body behavior as a one-way street; it's not. The way you control your body can affect the way you think about yourself. Using power poses will make you feel confident and powerful in your mind. The stance Wonder Woman takes, with her hands on her hips, can help you with this.

Before you take the stage or enter a meeting, put yourself in the Wonder Woman stance or a similar power pose for two minutes, because adding this to part of your preparation routine will give you the confidence boost you need. You may not feel the change as it occurs, but your body will. Power poses work on a physical level — your body automatically responds as it forms links between your body's stance and how the shape of your body matches the emotions you should feel. We shrink and fold our arms around ourselves when we feel scared or insecure because our body takes a stance of protection; we open our arms and legs up when we feel confident. The body literally projects itself into a power pose, and a power pose tells your mind you can do it.

Similar to the belief that our mind affects the body, but not vice versa, it is commonly misconceived that the use of body language only applies to you, the speaker, during a presentation. This would be like only looking at one side of a chess board during a game. It is the relationship between the two sides of a chess game, between the speaker and the audience, how these pieces interact and influence each other, that matters. If you only focus on one side, you miss vital information that you need to understand the other side, and you will lose the ability to take a step back and see your game (or your performance) as a whole.

However, just like in chess, the movements you make matter and create certain effects. Here are helpful techniques to consider when it comes to body language to help you own the room:

- Use a warm smile as you are introduced or introduce yourself.

- Initially keep your arms at your side or clasped in front of you.

- Do not overuse your arms and hands during your presentation — keep gestures purposeful so that you use them to emphasize a point.

- Do not lean on a podium — this is perceived as weakness.

- Include the entire room in your use of eye contact, so people sitting in a certain section do not feel neglected.

- Use appropriate facial expressions to match your points (for example, raise your eyebrows if you share a story about being surprised, or take a somber expression while talking about a serious subject matter).

- Use purposeful movement if you walk around on stage — step forward to introduce a point, to the side for transitions, and backwards to conclude a point.

- Eliminate body movements associated with anxiety, including swaying back and forth on your feet, wringing your hands, crossing your arms over your chest, or touching your neck.

- Keep in mind the truism, "Movement is always good, but it must be movement with purpose."

- If you are in a position where you must sit, leaning forward towards other people can convey friendliness.

Take these strategies and use them to improve your presentation skills, but also take this knowledge and use it as a tool to understand your audience as you interact with them. Keep your eyes open as you talk and analyze your audience's body language. These clues will help you to interact with people in a meaningful way, since you can use techniques such as these to keep people engaged. As you begin, it may be helpful to look up video clips of your favorite presenters to study their use of body language, so you can see these strategies in action and imitate them as you learn them.

I am sure you've heard the phrase, "Be the change you want to see." When it comes to body language, you could say, "Use the body language you need to create the impact you want to see." Body language is a skillset readily available for you to conquer. Start with one or two strategies and incorporate them until you are comfortable to try the next. Your body and mind can work together, and you will become a master at putting both to use.

Chapter 40: Using Visuals

"If you tell me, it's an essay. If you show me, it's a story."
—Barbara Greene

One thing that can be tremendously helpful in giving a presentation is the use of visual aids. This added strategy, however, is a little harder than it may seem. It is far too easy to look incredibly unprofessional if you use subpar visuals, but when done right, they can and will vastly improve your presentation.

How many times have you heard the phrase, "A picture is worth a thousand words"? People have short attention spans. We're easily distracted, and we're easily annoyed. Large blocks of text can be hard to focus on for any significant period of time and, unless you're an exceptionally dynamic speaker, focusing on your voice can be equally hard. Make it easier. Make it more interesting. Use pictures to draw people's attention to your points.

It's not all about inserting images, though. The whole presentation needs to be aesthetically pleasing. This means focusing on colors and font sizes, too. It also means not going overboard.

Simplicity and consistency are vital. Don't try to show too much, and try not to show anything that isn't necessary. Will it make your material more understandable? Use it. Will it make your material more interesting? Use it. Will it show off how good you are with technology? Don't use it. Will it make your presentation significantly longer? Don't use it. Will it distract from the point you're making? Definitely don't use it.

You're an intelligent person. Exercise good judgment here. Technology can be exciting, and it's always tempting to mess around and try new things, but you don't need to cram every new feature into a single presentation. Leave room for the content itself. That should always be the focus.

So how do you make that happen? Start here:

- Use fonts that are easy to read.

- Use large print.

- Don't put up many words, and make sure any sentence you use is fairly simple. Save the big words for the verbal part of the presentation.

- Don't use too many fonts.

- Pick visuals that fit together well.

- Think about each visual aid you consider incorporating, whether it's a graph, photo, video, or something else. Why do you want to use it? What will it add to the presentation?

- If you aren't using many visuals, try to spread them throughout the presentation to maintain interest, rather than cramming them all into one topic or area.

- Don't make your visuals more interesting than your topic. (This means interesting topics, not boring images.) The visuals should enhance your presentation, not overshadow it.

- Remember that the bulk of your message should be in what you're saying, not in a slide show. The visual aspect of the presentation should be simple, concise, and straightforward.

- Don't use anything you don't have the rights to.

- Make sure all of the information is correct, especially in visual aids that you did not personally create, or that you're reusing from a previous presentation.

Visuals add a lot to any presentation, on both ends. They're fun to see for the audience, and they're fun to put together. Be careful and professional, but let yourself have a good time, too. Adding visuals to your presentation will make it easier for your audience to understand and engage with, and it will improve it as a whole.

Chapter 41: Powerpoint Tips

"If anything, PowerPoint, if used well,
would ideally reflect the way we think."
—Steven Pinker

owerPoints are an effective tool to use to help people understand what you think. Emma Stone, a famous actress, used one to tell her parents that she wanted to become an actress. With her successful career, it clearly worked. Visual aids are easy to make, but creating a visual that is powerful, clear, and precise can be tough.

There are plenty of ways to create a presentation. You don't always have to use Microsoft PowerPoint. Websites online allow free slide presentation makers and many of them promote the finished products on their websites.

After deciding what program you want to use, there are key choices to make in preparing the slideshow for presentation.

- What message do you want to convey? Plan out what you want to say. Creating an outline helps immensely and should be done before putting the slides together. It also gives you a chance to figure out what you are going to say during your presentation.

- Who is your audience? If you are speaking in front of a group of professionals, odds are you don't want cartoons on your slides. If you are speaking to a group of teens or even college student-aged people, then cartoons may speak to them better. Spend time assessing who your message is going out to in order to create the proper slides.

- Keep it simple. Clean and simple slides are the way to go when creating your presentation. A rule of thumb you should use when you are getting the slides together is to make sure that you are not putting all of your information onto the slides. The slides are just meant to be used as a visual aid, not for you to read your whole presentation from. It's okay for you to reference back to it for emphasis or explanation, but the majority of your slides should only show enough information for your audience to take notes.

- Think about color. When using color in slides, think about the emotions you want the audience to feel. If you want them to feel calm, use blue; for confident, yellow. Color psychology is used in advertising and many other mediums; why not in your presentation? An easy internet search will give you plenty of options in understanding what colors to use. The rule of thumb to follow with text is to keep the colors low intensity. Black text on light backgrounds and white text on dark backgrounds usually works rather well.

- Think about emotion. Empathizing with your audience is a great way to connect. Make your slides convey a little about you. Open up and share a bit of yourself in them. A great way to do this is with a story. Are you trying to sell a product through your slides, or a way of thinking? Tell a story. Stories make people relate to the information better and make you more personable.

Overall, PowerPoint can be a great tool to use in creating presentations. Having the visual aid makes the information you are sharing more concrete and easier to remember. Just don't rely on the slideshow to do all of your presenting for you and you will be great.

Chapter 42: International Differences

"To effectively communicate, we must realize that we are all different in the way we perceive the world."
—Tony Robbins

During your career, you will most likely do business with a wide variety of people, including people of different nationalities. This is not only exciting, but should also prove beneficial to both you and the person you are dealing with. Because of this, you must be cautious in order to not accidentally offend someone, or fail at getting your point across. The key, here, is to make sure that you will not come across as ignorant or offensive when interacting with others from different countries and cultures. Cultural references should be held to a minimum, for maximum understanding. While this may seem challenging, it is actually fairly easy to prepare yourself for this.

- Make sure to research different cultures in order to gain a working understanding of what is considered the "norm" to them. We all have our own set of customs and rules, and you should make it a point to brush up on these before your presentation.

- Make sure that you do not use any references that may be lost on people from a different cultural background. For example, referencing something that is specifically "American" in origin may not translate to people in Asia. Avoid this mistake by establishing a common denominator in your presentations or speeches that is universal to the room.

- Also be aware of various codes of conduct that may differ from culture to culture. Some may be far more or less formal than what you are accustomed to. Attempt to fit within these in regards to dress, greetings, and your general presence.

- Avoid anything that could be deemed offensive to another culture. Following the rule of "no politics, no religion" could also help you in this regard, in some cases. Take care to censure your words so that you come across as friendly, professional, and respectful.

Following these guidelines will not only help in your dealings with people, but it will also provide you with a better understanding of other cultures. Think of this as an educational project — one that requires you to do a bit of extra work in order to ensure your success. This will make you more respectful of other cultures, and it will paint you in a good light to others. Everyone desires respect, and taking the time to research and master proper protocol is key. Wouldn't you want someone to do the same for you? People respond positively towards noticeable, conscious efforts in regards to their comfort.

Also, you will want to make sure that you brief your partners or team on your research as well. You are responsible for, and represented by, everyone on your team, so having someone speak out of turn could be detrimental. Make sure you are all on the same page, and encourage them to do their own research, if need be.

However, do not sacrifice your presentation too much — there will be minor changes, but make an effort to keep your basic material the same, if possible. Focus on getting your points across clearly, and act just as you would at any other presentation, while keeping your research in mind.

PART VII

Bring It All Home

Chapter 43: Knocking It Out of the Park

"Almost everyone will make a good first impression, but only a few will make a good lasting impression."
— Sonya Parker

When you end a presentation or meeting, you want to end on a final note that inspires people. You want your client, your employees, or whoever your audience is to look at you and think, "This is my role model." Most important, you want them to remember what you've talked about and be excited to just think about it.

Do you remember the last inspiring presentation or speech you heard? What about it really caught your attention? Did it have a powerful closing? Chances are that one of the reasons this presentation or speech was so memorable was because it had a strong closing statement. To knock your presentation or meeting out of the park, and leave your audience glowing from your presence, you need a solid, relevant, and motivational statement.

What should you include in your stunning wrap-up?

- Don't use notes during the last part (look your audience directly in the eye).

- Include a call to action.

- Stay on track (you want to hit the message home).

- Make a lasting impression.

- Hold a Q & A (if there is one planned).

- Utilize an inspirational closing remark.

Using notes during the last part of your presentation will only take away from the impression you want to leave on your audience. Make sure you rehearse the last part as much as possible, so when you're closing your presentation or meeting, you're standing straight, looking everyone in the eye, and showing them that you mean business. When they see how enthusiastic you are about the topic or project, that enthusiasm will spread to them and catch fire.

Your call to action is your intent. What do you want your audience to do after listening to your presentation? Do you want them to start working right away on the big project for an important client? Do you want them to begin improving the company's culture? Make it clear what you want from them and give them a reason to want to be a part of your vision of the future. If you and the project inspire them, their work will reflect that.

As you deliver the final part of the presentation, you also want to stay on track. Do not divert your audience's attention or else you will lose them, or, even worse, confuse them. This is not the time to deliver a little anecdote that semi-relates to your topic. Anecdotes are for the beginning of a presentation or meeting. The end is for being quick and direct. Do not add anything new that will throw off your audience. Bring the point home. What are you trying to say? Your point should be clear.

Many leaders will agree that the most important part of your presentation or speech is what you say last. That's where you will make your impression stick with people because it's what your audience will remember most. Before you even think about how to close your presentation, think about the impression you want to leave. Then, based off that impression, write and rehearse a closing statement that will wow your audience. If you're unsure of your closing statement, go ahead and practice with someone and ask for his or her feedback, or even practice with multiple people.

Depending on the kind of presentation or meeting you're having, you might have a Q & A session. If you plan on including one, make sure you set aside enough time for people to ask their questions. The goal is to answer most, if not all, of them, though it largely depends on the size of your audience.

When the Q & A session finishes, don't walk away. Have a final statement prepared. This statement should include a final note or reflection about the topic that will impress your audience. If you leave right after the Q & A, it won't be as memorable. Take the time to rehearse that final sentence or two. It could make or break your presentation, and you want to knock it out of the park.

Chapter 44: Following Up on Successes

"Coming together is a beginning; keeping together is progress; working together is success."
— Henry Ford

L ife is ready to beat you down. In business, you will hear the word "no" far more than you hear the word "yes." You will have tough days, lackluster days, and even almost impossible days. As a leader, you will have times where you feel frustrated and stuck in a rut. There will even be days where you are doing well but the people around you are experiencing a rough day, and it will affect you. All of these situations that arise are why it is essential to follow-up on successes — because you achieved them despite all the obstacles you faced.

You know you work hard to accomplish your goals. Yet the world rarely brings itself to a halt to praise your success. In the same way that you must take the time to determine your goals and the steps you must go through to obtain them, you must purposefully set aside portions of time on a regular basis to follow-up on your successes.

Depending on your needs, how you schedule this time may look different than how someone else does it. Perhaps you spend an hour every month going back to revisit your goals, measuring how far you've gone to reach them, and then mentally reflecting on your growth. Others of you may want to send out a short email to your employees that describe a few positive instances in the last month. Some of you may not need to assess your successes each month; perhaps a conference meeting in the office each quarter to discuss your growth works best for you. In order to function as a leader, however, you need to praise your own efforts to boost your own morale and to keep your momentum. You need to celebrate your improvements and victories in your business.

Similar to the way that you require encouragement, so do your employees. If you want them to improve and better themselves, you must appropriately follow-up and praise their success when they do so. Why? People need positive reinforcements to instill lasting change, and this means you need to delegate time to acknowledge your employees' successes. It will keep them motivated because it affirms that the work they put in to improve your business and themselves was worth it. It makes them feel valued because you communicate that you notice and appreciate what they do.

The way you conduct your follow-up depends on you, but it must always point to your employees' growth. No matter the method you use to communicate with your employees (a one-on-one meeting, a phone call, a thank-you note attached to a pan of cupcakes, an email, an all-hands meeting, or an office party), your acknowledgement should be sincere and genuine, and it should be appropriate for the behavior it celebrates. Root the praise you give out in reality, because people won't believe you the same way if you over-praise them. Find at least one way (even if it's small) that the person put in effort to reach a goal. It can be anything from consistently showing up to work, to keeping a positive attitude, to a successful sales pitch to a customer. What matters is that you find something to sincerely compliment.

People need to know that their effort makes a difference. You need this to function as a leader and to exude executive presence. When you recognize your successes on a regular basis, you build up your own confidence. Equally important, identifying moments of success in your business adds to your employees' confidence in their work and in their relationship with you. In the world of business, with all the times you hear the word "no," it is beneficial to sound your own "yes!"

You worked hard. Celebrate the results and keep going.

Chapter 45: Getting Back in Touch

"Too often we underestimate the power of a touch, a smile, a kind word, a listening ear, an honest compliment, or the smallest act of caring, all of which have the potential to turn a life around."
— Leo Buscaglia

Whenever you make contact with someone, the nice thing to do is to get back in touch with them. What does this mean exactly? Getting back in touch is similar to a checkup in that you plan out a time to visit with someone. However, unlike a checkup that you would usually correlate with a dentist or doctor, a follow up has different correlations. Getting back in touch is seen as a friendly reminder and pitch for your business.

Most of the time, you do not want to get back in touch with a business prospect, past customer, or current customer before 24 hours has passed. A good rule of thumb is to wait a day or two before following up. You do not want to come across as pushy or irritating by contacting them too early. Instead, you want to come off as friendly and helpful.

When you decide to get back in touch, do so over the phone or through email. Some people have preferences as to the best way of connecting with them. Today, many people always have their phones on them. However, if you know this individual juggles a busy career, a subtle email will suffice.

When you start your conversation, mention how much you enjoyed talking to him or her during your initial meeting. If you met in a memorable place or remember having a common interest, bring this up in conversation and tell him or her that you appreciated that. This will help the business prospect remember who you are and ultimately make you more distinct in their mind.

Next, you want to be direct in the fact that you wanted to follow up with them. Do not beat around the bush and allow them to get lost in your conversation. Instead, be straight forward. If you have services, relay these to the individual and tell them specifically how you can help them or how you would like to help them.

Before hanging up the phone, be sure to share your contact information with them. This way, they can get back in touch with you in the near future. Do not forget a friendly closing, even if the potential business prospect is not interested in your services. You want to build a positive relationship with them and to leave a good impression for when a need of theirs does come up so they keep you in mind.

Unlike the cases above, not everyone will answer your call. At this time, you'll find yourself listening to their answering machine. Do not look at this as a loss. Leave a friendly message stating your reason for calling and let them know that you will be getting back in touch with them again. Some companies have a standard follow up policy where follow ups occur every week. Keep track of who you follow up with and who you still need to get back in touch with. This will help yourself stay organized as well as actively engaged in keeping up with potential business prospects that you do not want to lose out on.

Chapter 46: Retool and Improve

"To improve is to change; to be perfect is to change often."
— Winston Churchill

After working through all of these success strategies, the only thing left to do is go back and look at everything you have accomplished to this point. Looking back and reflecting helps you to gain perspective and new thoughts on how to build yourself a better future. In order to get better, you have to continuously change for the better. That means working on the things that are not working and re-strategize on what you need to fix.

- Reflect. What have you done right and wrong since applying some of the new steps you have learned? Make a list of all the things that you have been practicing now. What has worked? What are the changes you see in your business and personal life since starting the little improvements? Focus on the positive and only reflect on what's not working as a way to figure out how you can improve it.

- Small steps. The common phrase, "Rome wasn't built in a day," is a perfect example of self-improvement. You cannot expect to change every tiny mistake in one day. Start small. Pick one aspect that you want to improve for a month. Make a game plan using the new steps you learned to change it. If your productivity is down, look at how you can make just small changes to fix them and watch the changes.

- Compound on success. Once you have one small step fixed, move onto the next. While moving onto the next, be sure that you are still tracking the previous step. These small, compound effects will give you a far bigger result than if you would have tried to change everything quickly. Slow and steady wins the race, remember? There is a reason for it. If you try to change it all at once, you and your teammates will become overwhelmed and you will fall back into the same problematic habits you had prior.

- Encourage. Celebrate the wins. The fact that you are changing for the better is a fantastic thing. Take the little victories happily. You are improving and it takes a great person to improve what they are doing. Some people like fun gold stars; others like to take themselves to dinner when something positive happens. Every success, even the small one, is important to the growth of you and your business. Be proud that you are making the changes.

Only you can change your life and business. Each day is a new start and a new time to create a better environment and greater value of living. The best decision you can put into action is to create a positive atmosphere in your business that looks at each trial and tribulation as a learning experience. Did you have a mistake yesterday? Did you experience a failure? Okay. Great. Stop and reflect. What did you learn? Take those mistakes and failures as a lesson for how you can improve the next time you try. Truly successful people try again and again until they get it right. You can, too.

Chapter 47: Be Excited

"Nothing great was ever achieved without enthusiasm."
— **Ralph Waldo Emerson**

I t's hard to excel at something you hate. Let yourself enjoy your leadership. What goal can't you wait to achieve? What, when it happens at works, make you think you are going to have a great day? What do you want to be known for? Get excited about what you're doing! Get other people excited about what you're doing. A little enthusiasm goes a long way, and it starts with you.

Make your work into something fun. Reward success. Try new things. Take chances. Do your best to make your business the best it can possibly be for everyone involved. No one wants to follow someone who doesn't care. It's important to maintain your professionalism, but always preserve your passion, too. Let your followers know that you truly care — about them, about your cause, about your work. If you can't get excited about what you're doing, you should probably be doing something else.

You should be excited for yourself, but remember to create an atmosphere of excitement for everyone else, too. Listen to people. Be open to new opportunities. Throw holiday parties. Give bonuses. Tell everyone how great their work is — individually and as a group. Build passion and enthusiasm for your entire team. Create a group of people who love what they do.

We should all know how to enjoy ourselves, but here are a few tips for doing it as a leader:

- There are times when calmness is better. Avoid the kind of excitement that gets you into fist fights and heated debates. Don't be hysterical.

- Read the situation. Pay attention to what's going on. Is excitement the best course of action right now, or do you need to set a good example by being calm, steady, and solid?

- Don't try to fake your excitement. If you're genuinely happy about what you're doing, let it show — but don't lie to your followers. They'll probably see right through you, anyway.

- There's a difference between lying to your audience and faking it until you make it. If you don't care, don't pretend you do. But if you're just having trouble drumming up enthusiasm after a rough week, try to act excited until you start to feel it again.

- Let loose. Be animated. Pace, gesture, and let your enthusiasm show. Excitement is easy to catch.

- Be positive.

- Let everyone know exactly what you're excited about and why.

- Get excited about other people's good work.

- Do work that you love.

- If you're having trouble getting excited on any particular occasion, try drawing on your memories of the last time everything went well.

- Cultivate relationships with passionate people who will be enthusiastic about your work.

- Focus your enthusiasm on your team or on your goal — not on yourself. Your followers don't need to hear how excited you are about how well you did on the last project you finished. Don't make this about you.

- Be spontaneous.

- Create an environment where people are comfortable celebrating. Be a fun person to work with.

With passion and enthusiasm, you can go as far as you want to go. There's no point in leading something you don't care about. So enjoy yourself. Let others enjoy themselves. You're going to be an amazing leader. Get excited about it.

Chapter 48: 30,000 Foot View

"The future belongs to those who believe in the beauty of their dreams."
— Eleanor Roosevelt

Nothing is more powerful than a vision that is set in motion. What is your dream? Keep the big picture in your mind at all times, because there will be moments when building your dream will get tough. You will have hard times. You will fail at times but, in order to keep going, you must have a reason to never give up. You must have a concrete dream.

What is your dream? Is your dream to build a business as big as Apple? Steve Jobs did not start his business as a million dollar company. He built his vision from the ground up and, up to his death, he lived it day after day. If Steve Jobs would have given up, do you think we would have the amazing technology we do today? Maybe. But we really do not know if we would have the same rises and changes that we've acquired. Apple changed the face of phones, music, animation, and even computers — all from one man's dream. Is your dream something that could change the face of the world? It doesn't have to be as big as Apple, but having a dream builds all of us up and helps to motivate you.

- Create a vision board. Vision boards are great at reminding you of your dreams. Make it on the computer and put it as your desktop background. Set it as your tablet's screensaver, even your telephone. Seeing that every day will build that dream and give you motivation to keep going even when you think about getting up.

- Set goals. If you know that you have a big dream that you are nowhere near achieving, plan out small goals that you can achieve each day. At the beginning of the day, reflect on what you need to do to make the most of your day. At the end of the day, reflect on what you did that day to make it further. Always think about your day in terms of how you are moving towards that goal. Keep the big picture in your head when you plan out your day, and focus on those activities that get you there.

- Keep a journal. When you are reflecting, write down the successes and little steps you've taken daily to see the dream unfolding. Write down your changes. Write down the things you've learned about yourself or your dream. Be open to the small things that happen in your life when you open up for changes.

Remember, only you have the vision for your future. Not your colleagues, or your family, or your friends. You do. You are also the one who must keep your dream alive. Through your purposeful planning, you can change the outcome of the future. Do you want your future to be brighter and your dreams to come true? You have to continue to visualize. Not once, but daily. Those who constantly remind themselves of what they are aiming for will achieve their dreams. Will you be one of them?

Chapter 49: Be Grateful and Graceful

"Develop an attitude of gratitude, and give thanks for everything that happens to you, knowing that every step forward is a step toward achieving something bigger and better than your current situation."
— Brian Tracy

Once you've hit your stride and everything seems to be going according to plan, you may find yourself tempted to become cocky. This is natural — you've done so much! Look at what you've accomplished! Shouldn't you be proud of yourself? Of course you should. You should be giving yourself a pat on the back once a day. However, forgetting the people along the way, and not realizing how fortunate you have been in the face of all your hard work, is something to work against. Self-realization is a key step to take for any successful person, and it is incredibly important for you to keep yourself grounded, regardless of all the amazing things that may be happening.

We all know someone who seems to take things for granted, who doesn't seem to realize just how good they've got it. And how do you feel about that person? You probably don't like them much, and you might resent them a little. That attitude is what you will want to resist each and every time you encounter another success, and reap the benefits of your hard work.

There are a handful of ways to work against this, and we will detail them below:

- Remember the little people. This is so necessary. You must take a step back and recount all of the people that have helped you along the way. Appreciate their service to you—whether large or small—and make a point to reconnect at some point and thank them for their support and their kindness.

- Practice being grateful to everyone you encounter. Gratefulness is an active appreciation for a good or service, and it comes in many packages, but let's take this a step further. Regardless of the size of the deed, work to feel grateful for anything that benefits you, your company, your work, and your life. It can be simple things rather than complex things. But, re-focusing your attitude towards life, and training yourself to view the world through "grateful" lenses, will not only bring you much happiness but it will also endear you to others. We all want to be beloved, and the trick is those rose-colored glasses.

- Be graceful in everything you do. When we say "graceful," we oftentimes think of a ballerina or swan. But this isn't the sort of graceful that you should think of, exactly. Being graceful in life means practicing kindness, consideration, and empathy. For example, if you were verbally attacked in a meeting—say, someone said something callous or rude to you—your first instinct would be to snap back in return. However, the graceful way of approaching this situation would be saying something polite instead, and not lowering yourself to base meanness (however much you want to).

These attributes can prove hard to cultivate, especially if you already have a fiery personality. However, they are important to you and will help you maintain success, as well as help you grow as an individual and leader. And, of course, people will notice.

Oftentimes, leaders are thought to be tough, maybe arrogant, and probably not the warmest people. While you should take pride in your accomplishments, and practice a healthy sense of confidence, as well as be "tough" enough to survive failure, these attributes should not detrimentally affect your personality. Be modest as you are proud of yourself; be smart and strategic, but focus on finding the best and kindest way of dealing with problems and problematic people. Appreciate how far you have come and the people that have helped you get there. If a problem arises, attempt to deal with it in a gentle, composed way. Remembering these two attributes will get you far, and drastically improve your outlook on life and the relationships you make in it.

TOOLS

3D PRESENTATION PLANNER

GETTING STARTED

What kind of presentation am I making?

What are the goals of my presentation?

What do I want the audience or client to think, feel, do or remember?

DATA

What needs or issues does the audience or client face that I will address?

How will I meet these needs?

What research do I need to do to be fully prepared?

DELIVERY

How will I open well? How will I confirm the agenda and time? How will I elicit from the audience or client their key areas of emphasis?

What are the key points to be included in the body of my presentation?

How will I close well with a compelling call-to-action?

DIALOGUE

What questions should I ask the audience or client?

What questions do I anticipate they may ask?

What issues may be unspoken that I need to surface?

Seven best Practices for PowerPoint Design

1. Be Consistent: use a consistent color scheme and framework throughout the entire slide presentation. Yellow fonts on a dark blue background are easy to read. If you don't have a corporate standard slide deck, this is a good template to adopt.

2. Keep it Simple, part 1: keep transitions and animations simple and consistent: No "cute" spinning or flashing animations in a professional slide deck. Since the Western eye reads left-to-right, bringing in all written bullets from the right-to-left allows for the easiest reading and comprehension. (This typically applies even in non-Western business presentations, since most cross-cultural business is done in English.)

3. Keep it Simple, part 2: practice the rule of 7x7x1: No more than seven bullets slide, each bullet no more than seven words long, with no more than one visual per slide.

4. Keep it Simple, part 3: keep the fonts simple and large: sanserif fonts for headlines (Arial, Helvetica, etc.), serif fonts for body copy (Times, Garamond, etc.). Use the same one or two font families throughout all the pages. By adding bold and italic, you can create visual interest and focus while still using a consistent font family. FYI: avoid using red as a font. The human eye has a hard time focusing on detail when it is in red — save red for arrows and circles to draw attention to specific items on a slide.

5. Bigger is always better: one powerful visual is always better

than several small visuals. The smallest font on the slide should be no smaller than 20 points. Leave plenty of "white space" on the slide; some experts say as much as 60% of your slide should be empty. It makes the content on your slide easier to focus on.

6. Focus our Attention, part 1: control the content on each slide by building reveals for each bullet you plan to discuss. Since most of us are visual learners, as soon as you show us a slide, we are going to read the whole slide; therefore, only show us one bullet at a time.

7. Focus our Attention, part 2: if you must share charts, spreadsheets or diagams on slides, use reveals with arrows, circles and larger, bolder fonts to direct our eyes to where we should focused our attention.

Seven best Practices for PowerPoint Delivery

1. You are the Most Important Visual, part 1: as a living, breathing, 3-dimensional communicator, you will always be more powerful than a 2-dimensional slide deck. Use the "B" key, which blacks out the current slide, to draw attention back to you. (Make sure your remote has a function key that allows you to do the same with a remote.)

2. Audience Rule-of-Thumb: if you are presenting to more than four people, you need to use a projector or large-screen monitor. Only present on your laptop screen for groups of four or less.

3. Use a Remote: use a remote, even for a presentation to a small group, so that you don't have to pay attention to the keyboard. Get a dedicated presentation remote — a wireless mouse is not as simple to use, and a wireless mouse doesn't typically have the "B" button functionality, mentioned above. FYI: do not use the laser pointer built into many remotes — the dot is too small to be seen clearly, and because it is hard to hold in one spot on the slide, it will magnify any nervousness you may have. Instead, gesture with your arm and an open hand.

4. Don't read from your slides: print off a pdf of your slide deck ahead of time 6-to-a-page, and use it as your notes. Remember: you are in charge of your slides, not vice-versa. Use your notes and the "B" button to keep the presentation as a conversation between you and your audience, with the slides simply providing support to your mastery of the material.

5. You are the Most Important Visual, part 2: stand to the left of the slide as you cover it. Since the western eye reads from left-to-right, we start our understanding on the left — you should be the first thing we look at, not the slide.

6. Test your technology ahead of time: in order to see if there are any last-minute adjustments that need to be made, go through the presentation slide-by-slide with the equipment you will be using in the room where you will be presenting. Often, if you supply the Powerpoint deck to the audience organization and they load it on their own equipment, the fonts and spacing may adjust slightly. Therefore you may need to make adjustments on-the-fly. This is particularly true if you have videos embedded in your presentation. FYI: have a back-up plan if your technology fails. Bring hardcopy of your presentation for each audience member in case you can't use the projector for some reason.

7. If you are asked to hand-out the deck ahead of time: try to do so in sections, perhaps three or four slides at a time, so your audience does not read completely ahead. FYI: if this is a customer presentation, do not hand out the budget or pricing slide at the beginning of your presentation. Keep it as a separate handout to be distributed at the appropriate time.

www.ingramcontent.com/pod-product-compliance
Lightning Source LLC
Chambersburg PA
CBHW050500190326
41458CB00005B/1367